2nd EDITION

Skills in English

Speaking
Course Book

Level 2

Terry Phillips

Published by
Garnet Publishing Ltd.
8 Southern Court
South Street
Reading RG1 4QS, UK

First edition, copyright © 2004 Garnet Publishing Ltd.
Second edition, copyright © 2004 Garnet Publishing Ltd.
Reprinted with corrections 2005.

The right of Terry Phillips to be identified as the author of this work has been asserted by him in accordance with the Copyright, Designs and Patents Act 1988.

All rights reserved.
No part of this publication may be reproduced, stored in a retrieval system, or transmitted in any form or by any means, electronic, mechanical, photocopying, recording or otherwise, without the prior permission of the Publisher. Any person who does any unauthorized act in relation to this publication may be liable to criminal prosecution and civil claims for damages.

ISBN 1 85964 781 2

British Library Cataloguing-in-Publication Data
A catalogue record for this book is available from the British Library.

Production

Project manager:	Richard Peacock
Editorial team:	Nicky Platt, Lucy Thompson, John Bates, Katharine Mendelsohn
Art director:	David Rose
Design:	Mark Slader
Illustration:	Beehive Illustration (Roger Wade-Walker), Janette Hill, Karen Rose, Ian West
Photography:	Corbis (Caroline Penn/Patrick Ward), Image Source, Photodisc

Garnet Publishing wishes to thank the following for their assistance in the development of this project: Dr Abdullah Al Khanbashi, Abderrazak Ben Hamida, Maxine Gillway, Karen Caldwell and the Level 2 team at UGRU, UAE University

Every effort has been made to trace the copyright holders and we apologize in advance for any unintentional omissions. We will be happy to insert the appropriate acknowledgements in any subsequent editions.

Audio production: Matinée Sound & Vision Ltd.
and John Green TEFL Tapes

Printed and bound
in Lebanon by International Press

Contents

Book Map	4
Introduction	5
Theme 1: *Education, What Kind of a Learner Are You?*	7
Theme 2: *Daily Life, I'm Sorry*	11
Theme 3: *Work and Business, The Time Thieves*	15
Theme 4: *Science and Nature, Natural Cycles*	19
Theme 5: *The Physical World, Do You Know Your Country?*	23
Theme 6: *Culture and Civilization, Good Luck!*	27
Theme 7: *They Made Our World, Can You Speak Telephone?*	31
Theme 8: *Art and Literature, Joha and His Neighbour*	35
Theme 9: *Sports and Leisure, How Do You Play* Surakarta?	39
Theme 10: *Nutrition and Health, Truths and Myths*	43
Word Lists	
Thematic	47
Alphabetical	49
Tapescript	51

Book Map

Theme	Speaking tasks	Phonology	Oral skills
1 **Education,** What Kind of a Learner Are You?	Revision	Revision	• Revision
2 **Daily Life,** I'm Sorry	Apologising and accepting apologies	/f/ vs /v/ Diphthongs: /ɪə/, /eə/	• Asking about feelings • Expressing apology
3 **Work and Business,** The Time Thieves	My time thieves	Unstressed syllables	• Using signpost words and phrases • Giving simple informal advice
4 **Science and Nature,** Natural Cycles	Natural cycles	Consonant clusters	• Making an arrangement
5 **The Physical World,** Do You Know Your Country?	My country and another country	Unstressed syllables (Reminder)	• Comparing two things • Saying you don't know • Expressing certainty
6 **Culture and Civilization,** Good Luck!	Wedding customs in my country	Stress in words – patterns Consonant clusters – /ks/	• Talking about information you have heard • Talking about past and present customs • Talking about arrangements
7 **They Made Our World,** Can You Speak Telephone?	Giving and taking telephone messages	Sounds of *g*	• Speaking on the telephone
8 **Art and Literature,** Joha and His Neighbour	Telling a story	Regular past tense verbs Unstressed function words	• Narrating a story
9 **Sports and Leisure,** How Do You Play *Surakarta*?	A board game in my culture	Homophones *Can* vs *can't* (BrE)	• Explaining rules
10 **Nutrition and Health,** Truths and Myths	Revision	Revision	• Revision

Introduction

THIS COURSE IS THE SPEAKING COMPONENT of Level 2 of the *Skills in English* series. The series takes students in four levels from Elementary to Advanced in the four skills, Listening, Speaking, Reading and Writing.

In addition, there is a remedial/false beginner course, *Starting Skills in English*, for students who are not ready to begin Level 1.

The speaking component at each level is designed to build skills that help students take part in speaking in English in class and in tutorial groups.

This component can be studied on its own or with one or more of the other components, e.g., Listening and Reading.

The course is organised into themes, e.g., *Science and Nature, Art and Literature*. The same theme is used across the four skills. If, therefore, you are studying two or more components, the vocabulary and structures that you learn or practise in one component will be useful in another component.

Within each theme there are four lessons:

Lesson 1: *Vocabulary*
In the first lesson, you revise words from the theme that you have probably learnt already. You also learn some new words that you need to understand the texts in the rest of the theme.

Lesson 2: *Speaking*
In this lesson, you practise skills that you have learnt in previous themes.

Lesson 3: *Learning new skills*
In this lesson, you learn one or more new skills to help you with speaking.

Lesson 4: *Applying new skills*
In the final lesson, you use your new skills with another speaking task text. In most cases, the tasks in Lessons 2 and 4 have a similar structure, so you can check that your skills have improved.

Web support for SKILLS IN ENGLISH

www.skillsinenglish.com

Contact enquiries@garneteducation.com to obtain a password for access to full site information.

THEME 1 — Education: What Kind of a Learner Are You?

In this theme you are going to talk about learning and different kinds of learner.

Lesson 1: Vocabulary

You are going to learn some of the vocabulary you will need to talk about learning.

A Answer these questions in pairs.
1 What is your favourite subject?
2 Can you explain why you like that subject?
3 Which sort of activities in your studies do you enjoy?
4 Which sort of activities do you not like?

B Read the proverb. Discuss in groups.

> I hear and I forget.
> I see and I remember.
> I do and I understand.
> Old Chinese proverb

C Look at Figure 1.
1 Say the words in the circles.
2 What does the figure tell you? Discuss in pairs.

D 🎧 Read and listen to the text. Complete it with a green word in each space.

How do you learn? If you like pictures, graphs and charts, you are probably a _____ learner. _____ means *of the eyes*.

If you like talking about new information with your friends, you are probably an _____ learner. _____ means *of the ears*.

If you like using the library and the Internet to find new information, you are probably a read/write _____. In other words, you need to read things or write them to remember them.

If you always like to do things with your hands, you are probably a _____ learner. _____ means *of feeling and movement*.

If you like to do two or more of these things, you are probably a multi-mode learner. _____ means *method* or *way of doing something*, and multi means *many*.

Vocabulary:
- college (n)
- meeting (n)
- speech (n)
- studies (n)
- subject (n)
- year (n)
- aural (adj)
- kinaesthetic (adj)
- learner (n)
- mode (n)
- visual (adj)

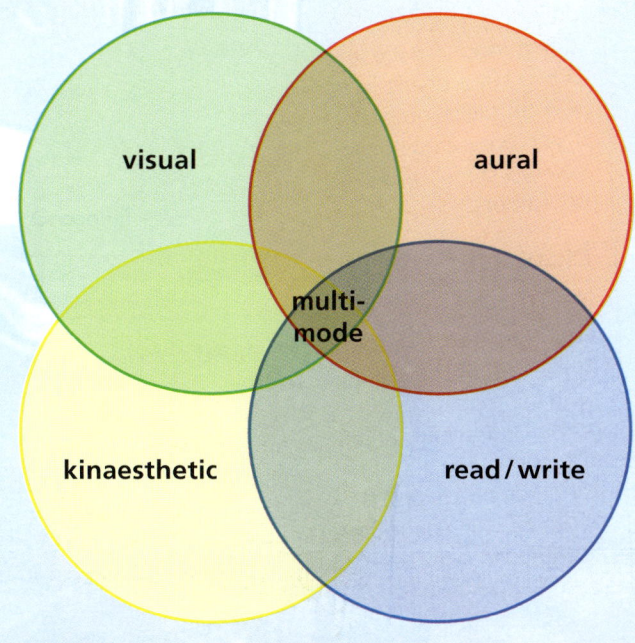

Figure 1: Types of learner

Lesson 2: Speaking

A Look at the page from a grammar book. Find:
1. the grammar point / tense.
2. the main example.
3. the exercise.
4. the cartoon.
5. the explanation.
6. the grammar table.

B Imagine that you don't understand the grammar point on this page. Would you …
1. look at the cartoon and grammar table and try to work out the grammar point?
2. read the explanation?
3. do exercises until you understand the grammar point?
4. ask an English-speaking friend to explain the grammar point to you?
5. do a combination of two or more of these things?

C Read the text below.
1. Do you agree with the description of your learning style?
2. Do you follow the advice for your learning style?

---

a

9 Present perfect 1
I've washed the car.

b

c
FORMS

Statements

I / You / We / They	have	washed it.
	have not	
He / She / It	has	finished.
	has not	

d Use the present perfect when something happened in the past, and affects us now.
  Tom **has cleaned** the car. (So now it's really clean.)
  Ann **has broken** her arm. (So now she can't write.)

e **3 Write these verbs in the correct forms.**
  arrive, break, catch, get, paint, win
  Example: Tom <u>has cleaned</u> the car. Now it looks like new.
  1 They _____ the TV. It doesn't work.
  2 The police _____ the bank robbers. They're at the police station now.
  3 Ann _____ the room. It's pink now.
  4 My parents _____. Their car is outside.
  5 Mark _____ the race. He's the new champion.
  6 Dad _____ the tickets, so we can go in.

So … what kind of a learner are you?

If you answered 1 to the question above, you are a visual learner.
2 = a read / write learner
3 = a kinaesthetic learner
4 = an aural learner
If you answered 1 and 2, or 3 and 4, etc., you are a multi-mode learner – like 60% or 70% of learners.

How can you improve your learning?
visual learners – use highlighters and coloured pencils for important information
read / write learners – read your lecture notes again and again, and write new information again and again
aural learners – discuss lectures with your friends and add extra points to your notes
kinaesthetic learners – after a lecture, try to think of real examples of new ideas

We use the present perfect when something in the past affects us now. For example, I've lost my watch, so I can't tell you the time.

Lesson 3: Checking skills

A The words on the left below are from Lesson 2. The words on the right have a similar sound.

1. 👓 Listen to each pair of words.

a	arm	am
b	read	rid
c	work	walk
d	main	mine
e	learn	lean
f	now	no
g	car	can't
h	wear	we're
i	try	tray
j	more	mall
k	she's	cheese
l	break	brick
m	like	lake
n	police	please
o	mode	made

2. Say each pair of words and make the sounds different.

B Are any words in Exercise A new to you? Work in groups. Ask about the meaning and pronunciation. If nobody in the group knows the word, look it up in a dictionary.

C Work in pairs. Say one word from each pair. Can your partner identify the correct word?

D The words below are all from Lesson 2.

> don't explain how kind like mode
> out page so table try

1. Put the words into four groups, according to the vowel sounds.
2. Check your answers in a dictionary.

E How will you remember new words from the lesson?

1. Tick one or more of these ways.
   ___ Write out the word several times.
   ___ Use coloured pens to highlight unusual parts of the word.
   ___ Draw a picture and write the word.
   ___ Say the word several times.
   ___ Make up sentences with the word.
2. Discuss your choice(s) in pairs.

Skills Check 1

Making yourself clear

Sometimes, two words only have one different sound.
Example: watch   wash
You must make the difference very clear when you speak.
I'm washing the car.
is different from
I'm watching the car.

Skills Check 2

Asking about new words

You should ask about the meaning of new words.
What's a brick?
What does brick mean?
Is brick the past of break?

You should also ask about the pronunciation.
How do you say this word: B-R-I-C-K?

If you can't ask anybody, look up the word in a dictionary. Try to recognise the symbols for the vowel sounds.

Group 1	Group 2	Group 3	Group 4
/eɪ/	/aɪ/	/əʊ/	/aʊ/
paint	write	go	now

Lesson 4: Applying skills

A Look at the text from a magazine.
1 Read the text.
2 🎧 Listen to two girls doing the questionnaire.

B Complete these sentences from the conversation.
Anna: Sorry, _____ do you _____ this word: D-I-R-E-C-T-I-O-N-S?
Maria: What _____ *collect* mean?
Anna: It _____ go and bring her to your house.
Maria: Let me _____. I _____ draw a map and tell her the directions.
Anna: OK. So _____ *a* and *b*.

C Work in pairs.
Student A
Look at Questions 2 and 4. Cover Questions 3 and 5. Ask your partner and tick the answers. Then uncover and ask Questions 3 and 5.

Student B
Look at Questions 3 and 5. Cover Questions 2 and 4. Ask your partner and tick the answers. Then uncover and ask Questions 2 and 4.

What kind of a learner are you?

Answer the questions. You can choose more than one answer in each case. Your answers will help to tell you what kind of a learner you are.

1 Your friend asks you for directions to your house. Would you ...
 a draw a map?
 b tell him / her the directions?
 c write down the directions (without a map)?
 d offer to collect him / her?

D Tell your teacher your partner's results. Your teacher will explain how to score the questionnaire.

2 You don't know how to spell a word. Would you ...
 a look it up in a dictionary?
 b get a picture of the word in your mind and write it that way?
 c say the word and work out how to spell it?
 d write the word several ways and choose the correct one?

3 Some English-speaking friends have just arrived in your town for the first time. Would you ...
 a take them on a drive around the town?
 b show them pictures and postcards of the town?
 c give them a tourist guide to the town?
 d tell them all about the good things in the town?

4 You are going to cook something for a special family day. Would you ...
 a cook something that you have cooked before?
 b look through a cookbook and find something that looks nice?
 c find a recipe that you have wanted to make for some time?
 d ask your mother to tell you a good recipe?

5 You are going to buy a new CD player. Would you ...
 a ask the salesperson to tell you about all the players in the shop?
 b read the information about each player?
 c test each of the players by using the controls and listening?
 d buy the one that looks the best?

THEME 2 Daily Life | I'm Sorry

In this theme you are going to learn how to give and accept apologies.

Lesson 1: Vocabulary

You are going to learn some of the vocabulary you will need to take part in the conversations.

A Talk about your everyday life. Use the red words.

B Work in pairs.
1 Read the article. Complete the text with one of the green words in each space. Make any necessary changes.
2 🎧 Listen and check your answers.

C Discuss these questions in groups.
1 When did you last argue with a friend?
2 Was the argument about possessions, words, feelings or something else?
3 How did the argument end?

D Find the multi-syllable red and green words.
1 Mark the stressed sound in each word.
2 🎧 Listen and check your answers.

E Which red and green words have the same vowel sound as:
1 hard?   5 fat?
2 feel?   6 here?
3 hot?   7 friend?
4 but?

breakfast (n)
diary (n)
dinner (n)
last (v)
period (n)
second (n)
angry (adj)
apologise (v)
argue (v)
argument (n)
calm (adj)
deal with (v)
matter (n and v)
sorry (adj)
upset (adj)
wrong (adj)

Parenting Magazine   September

Sorry – the best word in the world

Do you ever have _____ with your friends? What do you usually _____ about? Research by this magazine shows that most _____ between young children are about possessions.

That's my pen. No, it isn't. It's mine.

But as children get older, the cause of arguments changes. Most arguments between teenagers are about words or feelings. *You said I was stupid!* No, I didn't. *Yes, you did. You told Fernando Vasquez that I was stupid and childish.*

It is natural to be _____ by an argument, but you should try not to get _____. If you stay _____, it is much easier to _____ the problem. Ask your friend:

What's _____? or *What's the _____?*

Once you know the cause, _____ – even if you didn't mean to do it. Just say, 'I'm _____.' It is very hard to stay _____ with someone who _____.

Lesson 2: Speaking

A Vera Ferry is reading a magazine in the college cafe. She is reading about friendship and arguments.
1. Read the first part of the article – *The Problem*.
2. What do you normally do in this situation?
3. Which of the five choices is the best one?

B 🎧 Vera's friend, Phyllis, comes into the cafe. Listen to the conversation. Which of the actions in Exercise A does Vera choose?

C Read Phyllis's sentences from the conversation.
1. What does Vera reply in each case?
2. 🎧 Listen again and check your ideas.
3. Practise the conversation in pairs.

Phyllis:	Morning, Vera. How are you?
Vera:	_____
Phyllis:	What's wrong?
Vera:	_____
Phyllis:	Come on. Tell me. What's the matter?
Vera:	_____. Nothing.
Phyllis:	There is something. Are you angry with me?
Vera:	_____
Phyllis:	Yes, you are.
Vera:	_____
Phyllis:	Tell me what's wrong.
Vera:	_____
Phyllis:	OK.

D Read the second part of the article – *The Solution*. Which choice does the writer think is the best one? Explain your answer.

E 🎧 Listen to another conversation between Vera and Phyllis.
1. Which of the actions in Exercise A does Vera choose this time?
2. What happens?

F 🎧 Listen again to Phyllis's sentences in the second conversation. What does Vera reply in each case?

The Problem

Your friend does something you don't like. What do you do?
a Ignore it and hope it doesn't happen again.
b Telephone your friend and get very angry.
c Write a note, e-mail or text message and send it to your friend immediately.
d Visit your friend and explain how you feel.
e Don't tell your friend the problem, but make it very clear you are angry.

The Solution

Firstly, remember that problems between you and your friend don't usually go away by themselves. You have to talk about them. Perhaps your friend does not realise that he or she did something to upset you. If so, it may happen again.
Secondly, never confront your friend when you are angry. Calm down and think about the problem for a little while. Don't say or write anything that you will regret later.
Thirdly, it is best to deal with problems in conversation, not writing. Perhaps your friend wants to explain his or her side of things, but don't phone! Your friend needs to see that you are upset.
The best solution is to talk to your friend face to face and share your feelings. Don't get into another argument about who said or did what. Just tell your friend how you feel.

Lesson 3: Learning new skills

A Read the conversation below between two friends.
1. Complete the conversation with a suitable word in each space.
2. Read Skills Checks 1 and 2.
3. 🎧 Listen and check your ideas.
4. Practise the conversation in pairs.

   A: What's _____?
   B: It's _____.
   A: What's the _____?
   B: It's not _____.
   A: _____ you angry with me?
   B: No. Just _____ it.
   A: You have to _____ me what's wrong.
   B: OK. You were rude to me.
   A: I'm _____. I didn't _____ to be rude.
   B: You _____ I was stupid.
   A: I'm _____ sorry. It was a silly thing to _____.
   B: I'm not stupid.
   A: I know. I _____ say it again.

B What is the missing sound from each word below? How do you spell it?
1. Write something in each space.
2. 🎧 Listen and check your ideas.
3. Read Skills Check 3.
4. Practise saying the sentences with the correct sounds.

   a The con___ersation is between ___era___erry and her ___riend, ___yllis, in the ca___e.
   b ___yllis made ___un o___ ___era.
   c Tele___one and get ___ery angry.
   d ___isit and explain how you ___eel.
   e You ha___ to talk ___ace to ___ace about your ___eelings.

C Read these words from Lesson 2.

   | where | clear | id**ea** | pair |
   | r**ea**lise | really | share | there |

1. Put the words in two groups according to the (underlined) vowel sounds.
2. Read Skills Check 4. Check your answers.
3. Practise saying the words aloud.

Skills Check 1

What's wrong?

When we realise something is wrong, we often ask the other person to explain.

What's	wrong? / the matter?
Are you	angry with me?
	upset?
	worried about something?
Tell me	what's wrong. / what's the matter.

Sometimes the person doesn't explain.
Forget it.   It doesn't matter.
It's nothing.   It's not important.

Skills Check 2

Apologising

When we apologise, we use *I'm (really) sorry.* Then we usually add some more words.

Apology	Extra words
I'm sorry.	I didn't mean to say it.
	It was a silly thing to say.
	I won't do it again.

Skills Check 3

Saying consonants – /f/ and /v/

We make two consonants in English with the top teeth and bottom lip. One sound is soft, the other is harder.
1. The soft sound is usually written with *f*: *friend, feel*, but it can be written with *ph*: *phone, photo*.
2. The hard sound is usually written with *v*: *very, visit*, but it can be written with *f*: *of*.

Note: *have* has the sound /v/, but *have to* has the sound /f/.

Skills Check 4

Saying vowel sounds – /ɪə/ and /eə/

The vowel sounds in *here* and *there* are very similar. Make sure you can say the two sounds clearly.
Examples:
/ɪə/: *here, realise, really, idea*
/eə/: *there, share, pair, care*

SPEAKING SKILLS LEVEL 2 – THEME 2: Daily Life, I'm Sorry

Lesson 4: Applying new skills

A Work in pairs. Say the words and phrases below. Make sure your partner can hear the difference.

1	fan	van	
2	feel	veal	
3	ferry	very	
4	fill	villa	
5	fizzy	visit	
6	few	view	
7	life	live	
8	My wife's	My wives	
9	I have to go	I have two goes	
10	here	hair	
11	rarely	really	
12	ear	air	
13	fear	fair	
14	we're	where	
15	cheer	chair	

B Ask the teacher about the meaning of any new words and phrases in Exercise A.

C Practise saying these sentences.
1 Where's my wife's earring?
2 I have a few photos of the villa.
3 We have to visit Vera Ferry very soon.
4 Where we're going there are few chairs.

D Here is another conversation with an apology.
1 Match the statements and responses.
2 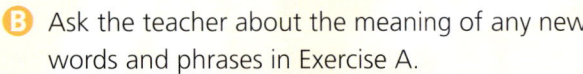 Listen and check your ideas.
3 Practise the conversation in pairs.

   a Morning, how are you?
   b What's wrong?
   c Come on. What's the matter?
   d Why are you upset?
   e You broke my pen!
   f Then you said it was a stupid pen anyway.
   g Yes, it was. It upset me.
   h Will you get me a new pen?
   i OK. I forgive you.

1 I told you. Nothing.
2 I'm really sorry. It was a silly thing to say.
3 I'm really, really sorry. I won't do it again.
4 I'm sorry. I didn't mean to break it.
5 Nothing.
6 Of course.
7 Thanks.
8 You made fun of me.
9 Fine.

E Work in pairs.

Student A
You have said or done something to upset Student B, but you don't know what. Find out and apologise.

Student B
Student A has said or done something to upset you. You don't want to tell Student A at first, but finally you tell him / her. You don't want to accept the apology at first, but finally you do.

THEME 3 Work and Business · The Time Thieves

In this theme you are going to talk about managing your time, especially when you are working on your own.

Lesson 1: Vocabulary

You are going to learn some of the vocabulary you will need to talk about managing your time.

A Discuss these questions. They use some of the red words.
1 What does a *telesales clerk* do?
2 Where do you find a *checkout operator*?
3 When do you need a *guide*?
4 What is a *counsellor* at a summer camp?
5 Who does an *assistant* usually assist?

B Which of the jobs in Exercise A would you like to do? Why? Which would you hate? Why?

C Do you like working with other people, or do you prefer working on your own?

D 🎧 Listen to a short talk about working on your own. Then complete the text with a green word or phrase in each space. Make any necessary changes.

Do you find it difficult to _____ when you are working on your own? Can you just sit down and start work, or do little things _____ you all the time?
   I don't have a problem when it is something I enjoy – a good film or a good book, for example. But as soon as I try to do some work, something, or someone, comes along and _____ me. My mobile phone rings, or a _____ from college comes by for a chat.
   I try to _____ my time. I make a _____ most days. It is usually very long, because I didn't do all the things yesterday or the day before. I sit down at my desk, and immediately I feel hungry or thirsty, or I suddenly think of something _____ that I have to do.
   I must learn to _____ when I am working on my own. What can I do to improve my _____?

E Do you have a problem like the speaker in Exercise D? Can you give him any advice?

assistant (n)

checkout (n)

clerk (n)

counsellor (n)

guide (n)

operator (n)

telesales (n)

colleague (n)

concentrate (v)

concentration (n)

distract (v)

organise (v)

TO DO list (n)

urgent (adj)

Lesson 2: Speaking

A How do you organise your private study time?
Do you …
___ study every day?
___ study at the same time?
___ study in the same place?
___ study for the same length of time?

B What sorts of things distract you from private study? Make a list.

C Read the article about the Time Thieves.
1 Does the article mention any of the things on your list from Exercise B? Tick those items.
2 Do you have *extra* Time Thieves that the article does not mention? Add them to the article in the correct section.
3 Does the article have *extra* Time Thieves that distract you from studying? Add them to your list.

D Play *Beat the Time Thieves*!
Work in groups. Think of a solution to each Time Thief – including your extra ones.
- If your solution beats the Time Thief *now*, you will get one point.
- If it beats the Time Thief *forever*, you will get two points.
- For the *people* Time Thieves, if your solution does not *upset* anyone, you will get a bonus point.

The teacher's decision on points is final!

How to Beat the Time Thieves

Are the **Time Thieves** stealing your time?
You know the problem. You have to study for an assignment. You have two hours between lectures. That should be enough time. You sit down and start to work – then the **Time Thieves** start stealing your time …
Who or what are the **Time Thieves**? There are lots of them in everyone's life.

Some **Time Thieves** are **people**.
- The hard-working colleague — *She wants help with the latest assignment.*
- The friendly colleague — *He just wants to talk.*
- _____ _____

Some **Time Thieves** are **things**.
- The mobile phone — *It never stops ringing.*
- The TO DO list — *There are so many other things to do.*
- The blank sheet of paper — *How do I ever get started?*
- The untidy desk — *I'll just tidy it and then I'll get down to work.*
- _____ _____

Some **Time Thieves** are **inside yourself**.
- The hungry stomach — *I need some food before I can even think of studying.*
- The tired brain — *I can't concentrate without a cup of coffee.*
- _____ _____

Lesson 3: Learning new skills

A Cover the article in Lesson 2. Complete these Time Thieves.

1 The hard-working _____
2 The _____ colleague
3 The _____ phone
4 The TO DO _____
5 The _____ sheet of paper
6 The _____ desk
7 The _____ stomach
8 The _____ brain

B Here is the second part of the article about the Time Thieves. Match each solution to one of the thieves above. Write the correct number next to each Time Thief.

___ **a** A glass of water is better for concentration than a cup of coffee. You should take one into your study room so that you don't have to get up and go and get one.

___ **b** Clear your desk, but don't deal with the things at this time. Put them in a drawer. You should tidy your drawer another time when you don't have to study.

___ **c** Don't plan to study at silly times of the day. You shouldn't try to study when you are hungry. Plan to study after eating a light meal.

___ **d** Just write something. It doesn't matter if you cross it out later. OR Start a spidergram with a key word from the assignment.

___ **e** Put a star beside important things. Put two stars beside very important things. Put three stars beside the important and urgent things. You should do the three-star things first, then study.

___ **f** Say that you will help her on this occasion, but explain that you usually study at this time.

___ **g** Tell him that you are studying – you will talk later.

___ **h** You should turn it off or tell people that you study every day from 1 p.m. to 3 p.m.

C You have a speaking assignment for the next lesson.

1 Read your assignment.

> **Assignment**
> What is the best way to beat the Time Thieves? Prepare a one-minute talk for the next lesson.

2 Choose four of the Time Thieves. Make a list in order of importance, e.g., *1. mobile phone*.
3 Read the Skills Check.
4 Make a sentence giving advice in each case. You can use ideas from Exercise B or your own ideas.

Skills Check

Giving advice

There are two main ways to give advice in English.

1	With the imperative	**Turn off** your mobile phone. **Don't plan** to study at silly times of the day.
2	With *should(n't)* + the infinitive	**You should turn off** your mobile phone. **You shouldn't try** to study when you are hungry.

Lesson 4: Applying new skills

A Read the multi-syllable words from Lesson 2 in the blue box. Put each word in the correct column according to the stressed syllable.
1. 🎧 Listen and check your ideas.
2. Check the stress in a dictionary. At the same time, check which letter(s) in the words have the symbol /ə/, if any.
3. Read Skills Check 1 to check your answers.
4. Practise saying the words with the correct stress and pronunciation of the unstressed syllables.

> anyone   assignment   concentrate
> decision   hard-working   organise
> serious   solution   studying   untidy

O o o	o O o
anyone	assignment

B Read the two-syllable words from Lesson 2 in the green box.
1. Mark the stressed syllable in each case.
2. 🎧 Listen and check your ideas.
3. Do any of the words have the sound /ə/?
4. Practise saying the words with the correct stress and pronunciation of the unstressed syllables.

> between   distract   friendly
> hungry   idea   lecture   mobile
> problem   study   tired   upset

C You are going to prepare your talk about the Time Thieves.
1. Practise giving your advice from Lesson 3 Exercise C. You can make a few notes, but you must not read the sentences. Make sure you stress the two-syllable words correctly and use /ə/.
2. Read Skills Check 2.
3. Add extra sentences to your talk.

D Give your talk. 🎧 Listen to the recorded talk. How could you improve your talk? Improve your talk and give it again.

E Are you going to take your own advice in future? What are you going to do to make sure that the Time Thieves don't steal your study time?

Skills Check 1
Unstressed syllables

What happens to **unstressed syllables** in spoken English? We often say them with the vowel sound /ə/. This can happen with any vowel letter, but it is not very common with the letter *i*.

Examples:
with *a*: org*a*nise
with *e*: *a*ssignment, conc*e*ntrate
with *o*: s*o*lution
with *u*: lect*u*re

Skills Check 2
Signpost words and phrases

When you want to speak for several sentences, you need to give the listener **signposts**. Signposts tell the listener something about the topic and the organisation of the information they are going to hear.

Examples:
I'm going to talk about how to deal with Time Thieves. (= Topic)
I'm going to mention four problems.
Firstly, …   (Advice 1)
Secondly, …   (Advice 2)
Thirdly, …   (Advice 3)
Finally, …   (Advice 4)

THEME 4 Science and Nature Natural Cycles

In this theme you are going to explain three natural cycles.

Lesson 1: Vocabulary

You are going to learn some of the vocabulary you will need to explain the cycles.

A You are going to talk about an experiment.
1. Read the description of *Method*.
2. Label the diagram with words from the description.
3. Discuss in pairs the *Findings* – what will happen – and the *Conclusions* – the explanation for the findings.
4. Try the experiment and check your ideas.

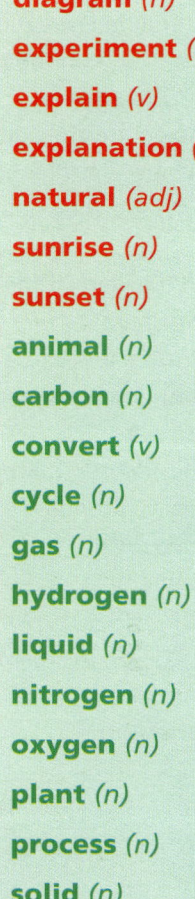

| diagram (n) |
| experiment (n) |
| explain (v) |
| explanation (n) |
| natural (adj) |
| sunrise (n) |
| sunset (n) |
| animal (n) |
| carbon (n) |
| convert (v) |
| cycle (n) |
| gas (n) |
| hydrogen (n) |
| liquid (n) |
| nitrogen (n) |
| oxygen (n) |
| plant (n) |
| process (n) |
| solid (n) |

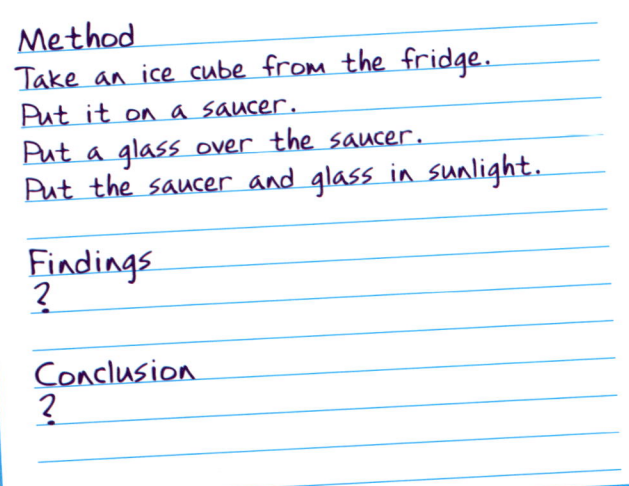

Method
Take an ice cube from the fridge.
Put it on a saucer.
Put a glass over the saucer.
Put the saucer and glass in sunlight.

Findings
?

Conclusion
?

B Work in pairs.
1. Read and complete the text with one of the green words in each space. Make any necessary changes.
2. 🎧 Listen and check your answers.
3. Test each other on the information in the text.

Natural Cycles

Three natural cycles keep the _____ and _____ on Earth alive. The cycles are the carbon and oxygen cycle; the nitrogen cycle; and the water cycle. All living things need _____ (O), _____ (C), _____ (N) and water, which is, of course, a combination of _____ and oxygen (H_2O).

    How does a natural _____ work? The _____ is simple. Something _____ or changes the form of a substance. Something else _____ it back again. For example, in the water cycle, the heat of the sun converts _____ water in rivers and seas into a _____. We see this gas in the sky as a white, grey or black cloud. Then, the gas cools and changes back to a liquid – called rain – or a _____ – called snow.

C Study Table 1.
1. Find examples from the text in Exercise B and copy them into the correct place in the table.
2. Think of more examples yourself and add them.
3. When does water change its state?

Table 1: Natural states of water

liquid	water,
solid	
gas	

Lesson 2: Speaking

A 🎧 Brenda Pride is calling her friend Trisha Crane on the phone. Listen to their conversation.
1 When are they going to meet?
2 Where are they going to meet?
3 Why are they going to meet?

B Read this part of the telephone conversation.
1 Write a word in each space.
2 🎧 Listen again and check your answers.

B: Hi, Trisha. It's Brenda.
T: Hello, Brenda. How are _____?
B: Fine. Well, _____, I need some help.
T: Of _____. What can I _____ for you?
B: Are you _____ this afternoon?
T: Yes, I think _____. What time is _____ for you?
B: What _____ two o'clock?
T: No, _____. I can't _____ it then. I've got a lecture _____ 3.00.
B: OK. _____ we meet at 3.15 in the college cafe?
T: Yes, _____. I'll _____ you at quarter past three.
B: _____. Thanks.
T: What's it _____?
B: I'll tell you _____.
T: All right. Bye.

C Practise the conversation in pairs.

D 🎧 Brenda and Trisha are meeting at the college. Listen to their conversation. Complete the information about Brenda's assignment.

E 🎧 Brenda is going to describe the water cycle. Listen and complete the diagram with suitable words in each box. Draw arrows to show movement from one box to the next.

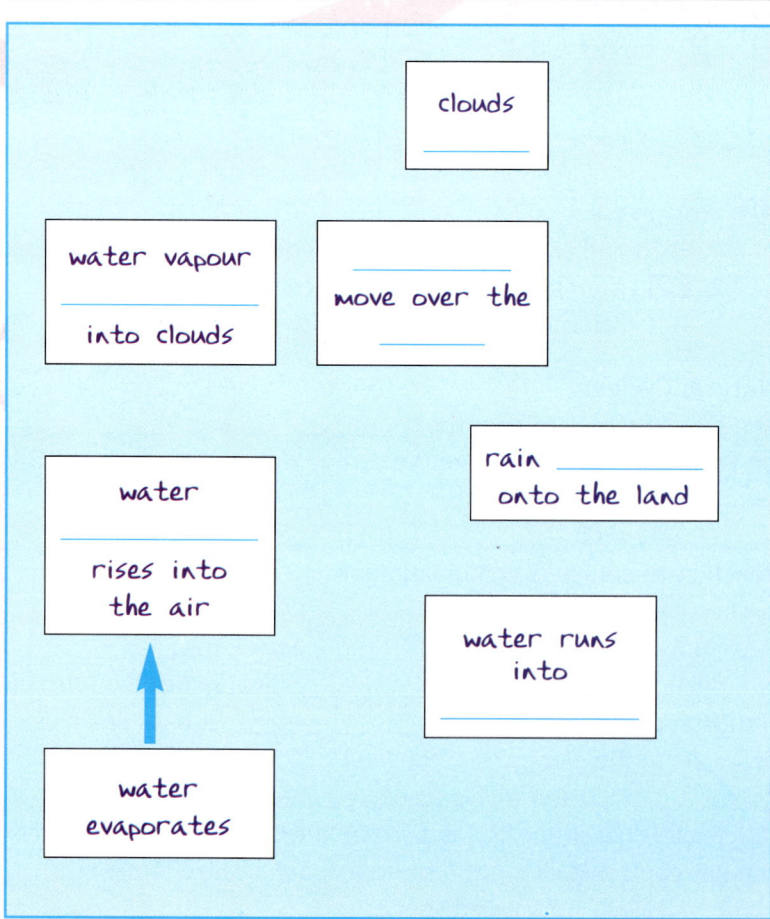

Greenhill College
SCIENCE FACULTY
Assignment 3

Prepare a short _____ (2 mins maximum) about a _____ cycle.
Choose one of the following:
• the _____ cycle
• the _____ cycle
• the carbon and _____ cycle

Explain any _____ words in the talk.
You will give your talk to some students from your group next _____.
Note: The students must be able to _____ the cycle from your description.

SPEAKING SKILLS LEVEL 2 – THEME 4: Science and Nature, Natural Cycles

Lesson 3: Learning new skills

A How do you make arrangements to meet someone?
1. Read the conversation. Work out B's question or reply in each case.
2. Read Skills Check 1. Check your ideas.
3. 🎧 Listen and check.
4. Role-play the conversation in pairs.

A: Are you free next week?
B: _____
A: What day is good for you?
B: _____
A: No, sorry. I'm busy then.
B: _____
A: Yes, sure.
B: _____
A: Can we meet at 12.00?
B: _____
A: Where shall we meet?
B: _____
A: OK. I'll see you on Thursday at 12.00 in the main entrance.
B: _____
A: I'll tell you then.
B: _____

B Make an arrangement to meet someone from your class. Use some of the language from Skills Check 1.

C What are consonant clusters?
1. Read Skills Check 2.
2. Find consonant clusters in Brenda's talk.

> I'm going to describe the water cycle. Can you try to draw it? Firstly, water evaporates from the sea. Evaporates is spelt E-V-A-P-O-R-A-T-E-S. It means that the water changes from a liquid to a gas. The water vapour – that's V-A-P-O-U-R – or gas, rises into the air. Then, the water vapour condenses. That's C-O-N-D-E-N-S-E-S. It's the opposite of 'evaporates'. In other words, it changes from a gas to a liquid. It forms clouds. The clouds move over the land and they rise. They cool over hills and mountains. The cold air can't hold as much water, so storm clouds form and rain or snow falls onto the land. The rainwater runs into rivers. The rivers flow into the sea and the cycle starts all over again.

Skills Check 1

Making arrangements

When we arrange to meet someone, we must fix:
- the day. • the time. • the place.

We sometimes also fix the reason for the meeting. Here are some of the sentences we use to make arrangements.

A	Are you	free	next	week?
			on	Monday?
			this	afternoon?
B	Yes,	I	think so.	
A	What	day	is good for you?	
		time		
B	Can we meet		on	Monday?
			at	3 o'clock?
A	No,	sorry.	I can't make it then.	
			I'm busy then.	
B	What	about	Tuesday?	
			quarter past?	
A	Yes,		sure.	
			that's fine.	
B	Where		shall we meet?	
A	How	about	the college cafe?	
B	OK.		What's it about?	
A			I'll tell you then.	
B	OK.		I'll see you at … on … in …	
A	Great.		I'll look forward to it.	

Skills Check 2

Consonant clusters

In English we can say some consonants together, without a vowel between. This is called a **consonant cluster**. Common clusters at the beginning of words are:

1. consonant + r   br, dr, fr, cr, gr, pr, tr
   Examples: from, draw, try
2. consonant + l   cl, gl, fl, pl, bl
   Examples: cloud, flow
3. s + consonant   st, sm, sn, sw, sl, sp, sc, sk
   Examples: start, storm, snow

D Practise saying Brenda's talk.

Lesson 4: Applying new skills

A Work in pairs. Follow the usual procedure with this activity.

Note: The words with capital letters are names of people or places.

1	approach	brooch	10	Gary	grey
2	Aston	stone	11	Terry	try
3	Callum	climb	12	Paris	price
4	Carrie	cry	13	pilot	plot
5	Derry	dry	14	below	blow
6	especial	special	15	support	sport
7	esteem	steam	16	sicker	skier
8	ferry	fry	17	asleep	sleep
9	follow	flow	18	parade	pride

stone

brooch

steam

frying

skier

B Work in pairs.
1 Choose one of the diagrams and texts below, A or B. Cover the other one.
2 Form groups of As and Bs. Look at the diagram. Read the text. Ask the teacher to help you with any of the words.
3 Go back to your partner. Describe the natural cycle to your partner. Try not to read sentences straight from the text. Draw the cycle that you hear. You can just write words in a box and join them with arrows.

A: The nitrogen cycle

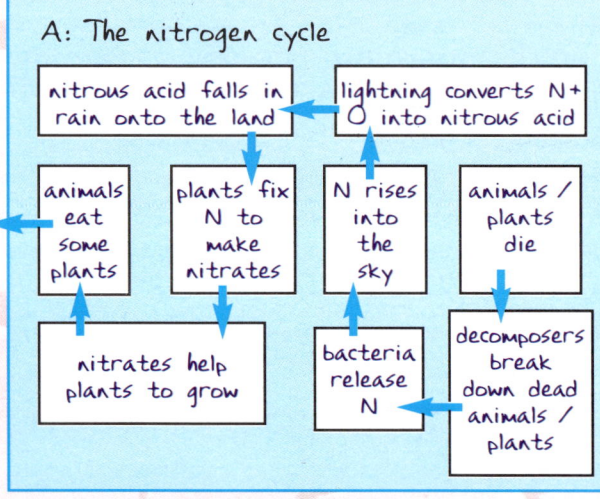

Animals and plants die. Decomposers break down the dead animals and plants. Decomposers are plants like mushrooms, and creatures like bacteria. Bacteria are very small creatures that live in the ground. We spell the word B-A-C-T-E-R-I-A. The bacteria release nitrogen. The nitrogen rises into the sky. During electrical storms, lightning converts or changes nitrogen and oxygen into nitrous acid. That's N-I-T-R-O-U-S. The nitrous acid falls in rain onto the land. Plants fix the nitrogen from the nitrous acid to make nitrates, spelt N-I-T-R-A-T-E-S. Nitrates help plants to grow. Animals eat some of the plants. The cycle starts again.

B: The carbon and oxygen cycle

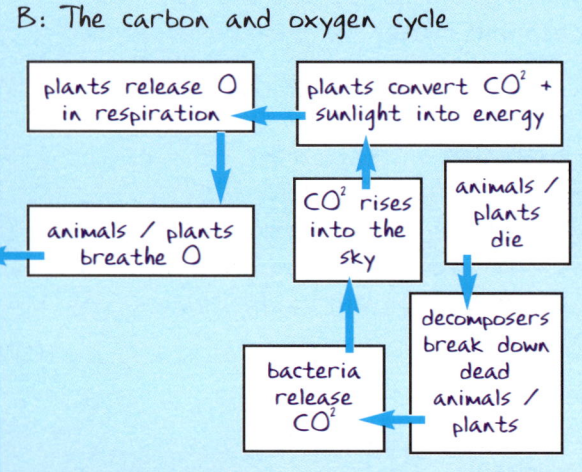

Animals and plants die. Decomposers break down the dead animals and plants. Decomposers are plants like mushrooms, and creatures like bacteria. Bacteria are very small creatures that live in the ground. We spell the word B-A-C-T-E-R-I-A. The bacteria release carbon dioxide. The carbon dioxide rises into the sky. Plants, especially trees, use carbon dioxide to convert or change sunlight into energy. At the same time, plants release oxygen, spelt O-X-Y-G-E-N. This process is called respiration. We spell that R-E-S-P-I-R-A-T-I-O-N. Animals and plants breathe the oxygen. The cycle starts again.

THEME 5 — The Physical World — Do You Know Your Country?

In this theme you are going to give a short talk comparing your country with another country.

Lesson 1: Vocabulary

You are going to learn some of the vocabulary you will need to compare countries.

A Find five continents in the red words.
1. Mark the stressed syllable in each word.
2. Practise saying the words.
3. Think of two countries in each continent.

B The Middle East is a **region**. Part of the region is in Asia and part of the region is in Africa.
1. Think of five countries in the Middle East. What is the name of each country in English?
2. Practise saying the English names, with English pronunciation!

C 🎧 Read and listen to the green words.
1. Mark the stress in each word.
2. Read Skills Check 2.
3. Underline the /ə/ sound in the words.
4. Practise saying the words.

D Read Table 1. Match each question to a green word in the table.
1. How big is it?
2. How many people does it have?
3. What's the weather like?
4. Where is the country?

Red words:
- Africa (n)
- America (n)
- Asia (n)
- continent (n)
- Europe (n)
- Oceania (n)
- the Middle East (n)

Green words:
- area (n)
- climate (n)
- location (n)
- population (n)
- region (n)
- temperature (n)

Table 1: The United Kingdom

Location	Europe
Population	59.8 m
Area	244,800 km^2
Climate*	warm, dry summers; cool, wet winters

*in the capital

E Study Table 2 for 30 seconds. Then test each other in pairs.
Example:
Where is the country?
It's in North America.

F Ask and answer questions about both countries.
Example:
Which country is in North America?
Canada.

Skills Check

Reminder
How do you say unstressed syllables in spoken English? You often say them with the /ə/ sound. Any vowel letter can make this sound in an unstressed syllable.
Examples:
with a: Afric**a**
with e: contin**e**nt
with i: reg**i**on
with o: Eur**o**pe
with u: temperat**u**re

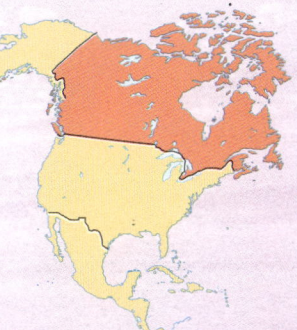

Table 2: Canada

Location	North America
Population	31.9 m
Area	9.9 m km^2
Climate*	hot, wet summers; cold, wet winters

*in the capital

Lesson 2: Speaking

A Dave Lines and Brad Jones meet in the corridor at Greenhill College.
1. Write one word in each space.
2. 🎧 Listen and check your ideas.
3. What arrangements do they make?
4. Practise the conversation in pairs.

   Dave: Hi, Brad. _____ are you?
   Brad: I'm _____.
   Dave: Are you _____ for a coffee?
   Brad: No, _____. I have a lecture now.
   Dave: What _____ later?
   Brad: _____ time?
   Dave: _____ about 11.00?
   Brad: Yes, I can _____ that.
   Dave: _____ we meet in the cafe?
   Brad: Yes, _____. See you _____.

B 🎧 Dave and Brad meet later. Listen to the conversation and answer the questions.
1. Why is Brad worried?
2. What is Dave's solution?

C 🎧 Listen again to part of the conversation.
1. What does Brad answer each time?
2. Read Skills Check 1 and check.

   Dave: OK. What's the population? How many people are there?
   Brad: _____
   Dave: Oh. OK. What's the area? I mean, how big is it?
   Brad: _____
   Dave: Oh dear. All right, here's an easy one. What's the average temperature in summer?
   Brad: _____

Skills Check 1
I don't know
We can say *I don't know* in several ways:

I	don't know.	
	have	no idea.
	couldn't	say.
		tell	you.
'm		not sure.

D 🎧 Listen again to the next part.
1. Complete Brad's sentences.
2. Read Skills Check 2 and check.

   Dave: Oh, come on! What do you *think*?! You've lived there for years!
   Brad: I _____ it's about 35.
   Dave: There. You do know something.
   Brad: Or it _____ be lower ...
   Dave: OK ... so 33 or 34 ...
   Brad: Or it _____ be higher ...
   Dave: What!?

Skills Check 2
Expressing certainty

I	think	it's	about 3 million.
It	might	be	higher.
	could		lower.

E Practise the conversation in Exercises C and D in pairs.

Lesson 3: Learning new skills

A Read these questions about a country.
1. Complete each question with a suitable word in each space.
2. Practise asking and answering the questions in pairs.
   a Which _____ is it in?
   b How _____ is it from the Equator?
   c _____ is the population?
   d What is the _____? How big is it?
   e How much rain do you _____ each year?
   f What's the _____ temperature in summer?

B Look at the quiz from the Geography Faculty at Greenhill College.
1. Write something in each section. If you don't know, write *?* If you are not sure, write c. in front of the information (c. = *about*).
2. Ask and answer in pairs. Use language from this lesson and the previous one.

> Which continent is your country in?
>> It's in Asia.
> What's the population?
>> I don't know.
> What's the average temperature in summer?
>> I think it's about 35 degrees C.

C Which adjectives go with each type of information? Write the adjectives from the green box in the correct place in the table. You can use the same adjective more than once.

D How can you talk about the information in the faculty handout?
1. Read the Skills Check.
2. What is the comparative form of each adjective in Exercise C?

E Talk about the information in the college handout. If you come from different countries, make sentences like Skills Check Example 1. If you come from the same country as your partner, make sentences like Example 2.

Greenhill College
Geography Faculty

What do you know about your own country? Complete the table with the information – or your best estimate of the correct information.

	My country	My partner's country
location		
continent		
region		
distance from Equator		
population		
area		
climate		
ave. temp. in summer		
ave. temp. in winter		
ave. rainfall in summer		
ave. rainfall in winter		

~~big~~   cold   cool   dry   far   high   hot   large   low   near   small   wet

area	*big*
population	*big*
distance	
temperature	
rainfall	

Skills Check

Comparing two things

We use **comparative adjectives** to compare two things.
Examples:
1. *Rainfall is **higher** in my country **than** in your country.*
2. *I think rainfall in the summer is **higher than** that.*

If two pieces of information are the same, we can use sentences like the following:
1. *Average rainfall is **the same** in my country **as** in your country.*
2. *I think rainfall in the summer is **the same as** you do.*

Lesson 4: Applying new skills

A Have you found out more information or the correct information about your country?
1. Add the new information to the table in Lesson 3.
2. Ask and answer again in the same pairs as Lesson 3.
3. Talk about the information again with comparative adjectives and *the same as* ...

B Study the information in Table 1.
1. Which things did you know already? Circle some of the information.
2. Which things didn't you know? Put a box around the information.
3. Talk about the things that you knew already.
   Example: *I knew Kuwait was very small.*
4. Talk about the things that you didn't know.
   Example: *I didn't know that the average temperature in Syria was only 17 degrees. I thought it was higher.*

Table 1: Facts about selected countries

	Syria	Egypt	Qatar	Kuwait	Oman
distance from Equator*	3,885 km	2,997 km	2,775 km	3,219 km	2,331 km
population	17.2 m	70.7 m	793,000	2.1 m	2.3 m
area	185,000 km²	1 m km²	11,000 km²	17,200 km²	309,000 km²
average temperature	17.0°C	21.0°C	26.6°C	25.6°C	28.6°C
average rainfall p.a.	187 mm	28 mm	81 mm	101 mm	75 mm

* to the capital

C Work in groups of four or five.

> **Student A**
> Choose one of the countries from Table 1. Don't tell the other students in your group. Answer their questions with only *Yes, it is* or *No, it isn't.*

> **Students B, C, D, etc.**
> Student A has chosen a country from Table 1. But which one? Find out by giving information about your country and asking Yes / No questions with comparative adjectives.
> **Example:**
> *My country is 2,750 kilometres from the Equator. Is your country farther than my country?*

D Choose a country from Table 1. Prepare a short talk comparing your country and the country you have chosen. Give information about all the items in the table.
Examples:
I am going to compare my country, the UAE, with Qatar.
My country is nearer the Equator than Qatar.

E Give your talk in small groups.

THEME 6 Culture and Civilization — Good Luck!

In this theme you are going to talk about marriage customs in your culture and other cultures.

Lesson 1: Vocabulary

You are going to learn some of the vocabulary you will need to talk about marriage customs.

A Discuss these questions. They use the red words.
1 What is the most important festival in your *culture*? Do you know any festivals in other cultures?
2 What is your date of *birth*?
3 What are the *special* dates in the calendar of your culture? Why are they special?
4 Do you believe in good and bad *luck*? Are you a *lucky* person?
5 Which of your *relatives* live in your house?
6 What do you think about *star signs*? Do you know your star sign?

B Look at the illustrations.
1 What is the connection between all the items?
2 What is the name of each item?
Clue: Look at the green words!

C Look at each group of words in the yellow box. They are all from Themes 1 to 5 in Level 2 Speaking.
1 Where is the main stressed syllable?
2 Say the words with the correct stress. Can you see any pattern? The blue word in each set is an exception.
3 Read the Skills Check and check your ideas.

Group 1	Group 2	Group 3
meeting	climate	colleague
learner	explain	matter
carbon	cycle	sorry
angry	counsellor	dinner
convert	apologise	assistant

D Practise saying the words in Exercise C. How many schwas (/ə/) can you find?

birth (n)

culture (n)

luck (n)

lucky (adj)

relative (n)

special (adj)

star sign (n)

bride (n)

ceremony (n)

get married (v)

groom (n)

marriage (n)

wedding (n)

Skills Check

Stress in words

As you know, you must learn the stress in new, multi-syllable words. There is no simple rule about stress within words, but there are common patterns.
Look for:
1 a long vowel – this is often the stressed syllable.
  Examples: 'speaking, 'argument
2 a diphthong – this is often the stressed syllable.
  Examples: civili'zation, 'process
3 doubled consonants – the stressed syllable is often the one before.
  Examples: 'marriage, 'wedding
Of course, there are exceptions to each pattern.

Lesson 2: Speaking

A 🎧 Gary and Sami are doing the same course at Greenhill College. Listen to the first part of their conversation.
1 What is Sami doing next weekend?
2 Why is Gary surprised?
3 What do you want to know next?

B 🎧 Listen to the whole conversation. How does Gary define each of these words?

> engaged exchange fiancée honeymoon
> wedding reception marriage

C Sami is a good language learner.
1 Make a list of things he does in this conversation to improve his English.
2 Read the Skills Check and check your ideas.

D Look at the parts of the conversation (A–E) below.
1 Complete Sami's sentences with one word in each space.
2 🎧 Listen again and check.
3 Practise the conversations in pairs.

Skills Check

Hear, check, use!
Every time you hear a new word, you should:
1 check the meaning.
2 check the pronunciation, including the stress.
3 use the word in the next sentence.
4 use the word 10 more times in the next week.

A
G: Because I didn't know that you were engaged!
S: What do you mean, _____?

B
G: In my culture, we exchange rings when we get engaged.
S: _____?
G: Yes, the man gives the woman a ring and the woman gives the man a ring.

C
G: Who is your fiancée?
S: My _____?
G: I mean, who are you engaged to?
S: _____ fiancée is called Dana. She's a student in the third year.

D
G: Right. Where are you going for the honeymoon?
S: _____ what?
G: The honeymoon. You know, that's the holiday after your wedding.
S: What is it _____?
G: A honeymoon.
S: _____ honey and moon?
G: Yes, exactly.
S: _____ is it called a honeymoon?

E
S: ... but the _____ starts at 6.00.
G: It's called a reception.
S: Reception. _____ in a hotel?
G: Yes, it's the same word, but it's got two meanings. It also means a party after a wedding.
S: Oh. OK. So the _____ starts at 6.00.

28 SPEAKING SKILLS LEVEL 2 – THEME 6: Culture and Civilization, Good Luck!

Lesson 3: Learning new skills

A Work in pairs.
Student A: Use one of the words from the yellow box in a sentence.
Student B: Imagine you have never heard the word. Be a good language learner!
Change roles.

> bride   engaged   exchange   fiancée   groom
> honeymoon   reception   wedding

B Read these sections from the conversation in Lesson 2.
1 Choose the correct form of the verb in italics in each case.
2 Read Skills Check 1 and check your ideas.

G: What …	
are you doing	next weekend?
are you going to do	
do you do	
S: I'm getting	married.
I'm going to get	
I get	

G: Where …	
are you going	for the honeymoon?
are you going to go	
do you go	

G: When is the reception?		
S: It	is starting	at 6.00.
	is going to start	
	starts	

C Work in pairs. Ask and answer about your arrangements and timetables for next weekend.

D The same sound is missing from each of the words in the yellow box.
1 Read the words and work out the missing sound.
2 Read Skills Check 2 and check your ideas.
3 Practise saying the words.

> ca__   e_tra   ne_t   si__   si__th   wee__
> e__ample   e__change   e__plain

Skills Check 1

Plans, arrangements and timetables

When we talk about the future, this often happens:
We make a **plan** – we *are going to do* something in the future.
The plan becomes an **arrangement** – we decide when we *are doing* things and where we *are going*, who *is coming*, etc.
The arrangements often contain a **timetable** – when the event *starts*, when it *finishes*, etc.
Example:

Plan	*I'm going to get* married next year. (I don't know the details yet.)
Arrangement	*I'm getting married* next weekend. All *my friends are coming*.
Timetable	The wedding *is* at 5.00. The reception *starts* at 6.00. It *finishes* at 10.00.

Skills Check 2

Consonant clusters (2) – /ks/

A common **consonant cluster** in English is *ks*.
This cluster appears in two situations:
1 with the letters *k* and *s*
   Examples: weeks, cakes
2 with the letter *x*
   Examples: six, example
The cluster often appears with other consonants to make three or even four consonant sounds together.
ks + 1   next, sixth, exchange
ks + 2   extra, explain

Lesson 4: Applying new skills

A Work in pairs. Follow the usual procedure for this activity.

1 Jack's	Jacky's
2 six	sixth
3 necks	next
4 Exeter	extra
5 This week isn't easy.	These weeks aren't easy.
6 The cake is nice.	The cakes are nice.
7 He didn't expel Anne.	He didn't explain.
8 Mike's books.	Mike has booked.

B Sami is talking to his friend, Ari.
1. Listen and complete the text with a word or phrase in each space.
2. Read the Skills Checks and check your ideas.
3. Practise the conversation in pairs.

Sami: I was talking to Gary the other day about weddings in Britain. _____, the man is called the groom and the woman is the bride.

Ari: Really? Do they have a party after the wedding, like we do?

Sami: Yes, _____ reception for the party.

Ari: Like the first office in a college?

Sami: Yes, _____ that they use the same word for a wedding party.

Ari: And do they go on holiday afterwards?

Sami: Yes. _____ a honeymoon. _____ a lot of couples ran away for a month – *moon* means *month* – until the bride's father was sweet again. _____, honeymoons are usually much shorter.

> **Skills Check 1**
>
> **Talking about information you have heard**
>
> When we talk about information we have heard, we often use special words and expressions. Here are some common ones:
> *Apparently …*
> *It seems that …*
> *I understand that …*
> *They call it …*
> *They use the word …*

> **Skills Check 2**
>
> **Talking about past and present customs**
>
> Customs change. We can show this with a word or phrase at the beginning of the sentence.
>
> | Past customs | At one time … |
> |---|---|
> | Present customs | Nowadays … |

C Work in pairs. Read your information about wedding customs in Britain. Then tell your partner. Use words and expressions from the Skills Checks on this page.

Student A	Student B
The best man At one time, the best man helped the groom to steal the bride from the bride's family. Nowadays, the best man is just a good friend of the groom. He looks after the rings. **The bridesmaids** Bridesmaids are young relatives of the bride. At one time, the bridesmaids were girls about the same age as the bride, and they all wore similar dresses. This was to hide the bride from evil spirits. Nowadays, bridesmaids are usually very young relatives of the bride.	**The wedding cake** This tradition probably comes from the Romans. They believed that cakes brought good luck. The bride and groom must cut the first slice from the cake together, then they will have children. They must keep a piece of the cake for one year, to bring them good luck. **The bride's bouquet** The bride carries a bunch of flowers called a bouquet. She throws the bouquet over her shoulder at the end of the wedding and the girl who catches it will be the next bride – according to tradition.

D Tell your partner about wedding customs in your culture.

E Tell the teacher about the wedding customs that you heard about from your partner.

THEME 7 — They Made Our World: Can You Speak Telephone?

In this theme you are going to learn about telephone language.

Lesson 1: Vocabulary

You are going to learn some vocabulary you need to talk on the telephone.

A Discuss these questions. They use some of the red words.
1 Where can you find a *captain*?
2 Are you a *cyclist*?
3 What is special about a *helicopter*?
4 Can you name any famous *inventors*? What did they *invent*?
5 What can you *ride*? Name at least ten things.

B Read and listen to Text 1. It contains some of the green words. Complete Figure 1 with a green word or words in each space.

Text 1

The telephone is a wonderful invention. It is easy to make a telephone call, but do you know how to talk about it in English? First you **pick up** the receiver. You hear the dial **tone**. You **dial** the number. If the line is **free**, you hear the ringing **tone** until someone **answers**. If the line is **engaged**, you hear the **engaged tone**. You have to **hang up** and **call** back later.

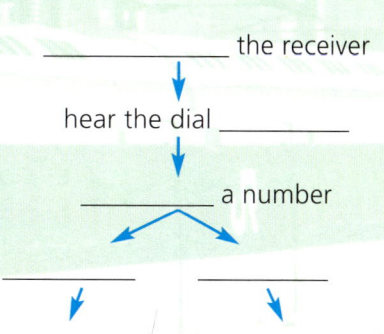

Figure 1: Making a telephone call

_____ the receiver
↓
hear the dial _____
↓
_____ a number
_____   _____
↓   ↓
someone _____ _____

C Read and listen to Text 2. It contains some more green words. Draw a figure to show the information in this text.

Text 2

If you call an organisation with a lot of telephones, your call will probably go to a **switchboard**. The **telephonist** will ask you for a name and **put** you **through** to that person's **extension** number. She will ask you to **hold the line**, which means 'wait for the person to answer'. If the **extension** is free, you can speak to the person. If it is **engaged**, you can **hang up** and **call** back later, or **hold** until it is **free**.

D Discuss these questions about your country in groups.
1 Telephone sounds are not the same all over the world. What is the sound in your country for:
　a the dial tone?
　b the ringing tone?
　c the engaged tone?
2 Who speaks first during a phone call – the caller or the person who answers?
3 How do you answer the phone? e.g., *Hello* or *Here* or *Ready*.

---

captain (n)

cyclist (n)

helicopter (n)

invent (v)

invention (n)

inventor (n)

ride (v)

rider (n)

answer (the phone) (v)

call (v)

dial (v)

engaged (adj)

extension (n)

free (adj)

hang up (v)

hold (the line) (v)

pick up (v)

put through (v)

switchboard (n)

telephonist (n)

tone (n)

Lesson 2: Speaking

A Match the verbs and the nouns to make telephone language.

1 answer	a a call
2 ask for	b a caller
3 dial	c a name
4 hear	d a number
5 hold	e a person
6 make	f the dial tone
7 pick up	g the line
8 put through	h the phone
9 speak to	i the receiver

B Abdulla gets lots of phone calls every day.
1 Listen to a call. What's the problem?
2 Read the conversation (Call 1).
3 Write a suitable word in each space.
4 Listen again and check your ideas.
5 Practise the conversation in pairs.

C Abdulla gets another call.
1 Read the conversation (Call 2). Think of a suitable reply for Abdulla in each case.
2 Listen and check your ideas.
3 Write Abdulla's replies.
4 Practise the conversation in pairs.

D Abdulla has to call Gary.
1 Why does he have to call him?
2 Role-play the telephone call.

Student A	Student B
You are Abdulla. Call Gary's house. Give Gary the message.	You are Gary. Answer the phone.

3 What can Abdulla do if Gary is out?
4 Role-play the telephone call.

Student A	Student B
You are Gary's mother or father. Gary is out.	You are Abdulla. Call Gary's house.

E Listen to Abdulla's call. What happens? Why?

Call 1
A: Hello?
C: Good morning. Is _____ Mohammed?
A: No, _____ isn't.
C: Is Mohammed _____?
A: Sorry. I think you've got the _____ number. _____ is a private house.
C: Oh. Is that 506-784?
A: No, _____.
C: Oh, I'm sorry.
A: It's _____. Bye.
C: Goodbye.

Call 2
A: Hello?
C: Good morning. Is that 506-748?
A: _____.
C: Is that Abdulla?
A: _____.
C: Oh, hi, Abdulla. This is Gerald, Khalid's friend.
A: _____.
C: I have a message for you from Khalid.
A: _____.
C: He says he can't come to the lecture this morning but he'll see you tomorrow.
A: _____.
C: Don't mention it. Oh, could you ring Gary and tell him? I don't have his telephone number.
A: _____.
C: Thanks. Bye.

Lesson 3: Learning new skills

A Do you know what to *say* on the telephone? Choose the best way to complete each piece of telephone language.
1. Is *that / this* Gerald?
2. *This / Here* is Peter.
3. Is Khalid *there / available*?
4. Khalid *speaking / talking*.
5. You've got the *wrong / bad* number.
6. I'm afraid he's *gone / out*.
7. Can I *take / have* a message?
8. Could you *tell / say* him …?
9. I can't hear you very *good / well*.
10. Could you speak *higher / up*?

B Do you know how to *reply* on the telephone?
1. What can you say if you hear each of the sentences in the green box? Think of something suitable.

> a I'm putting you through.
> b Can you hold the line?
> c The line's engaged.
> d Would you like to hold?
> e I'm trying to connect you.
> f Do you know the extension number?
> g Can I take a message?

2. Read Skills Check 1 and check.

C How do you say the letter *g* in the words in the yellow box?
1. Decide in pairs.
2. Read Skills Check 2 and check.
3. Check the pronunciation of *g* in a dictionary if you are still not sure.

> arrangement assignment colleague college
> engaged forget gas good groom hang
> message organise oxygen region ring
> sign speaking urgent wedding wrong

D Practise the telephone conversations from Lesson 2 again. Try to pronounce *g* correctly in every case.

Skills Check 1

Telephone language

If you hear …	you can say …
I'm putting you through. / I'm trying to connect you.	'Thank you' – and wait.
Can you hold the line? / Would you like to hold?	'Yes, certainly.' OR 'No, it's OK. I'll call back.'
The line's engaged.	'I'll hold.' OR 'I'll call back.'
Do you know the extension number?	'Yes, it's …' OR 'No, I'm afraid I don't.'
Can I take a message?	'Yes, please. Could you tell him / her …' OR 'No, it's OK. I'll call back.'

Skills Check 2

Sounds of *g*

The letter *g* makes three main sounds:

1 /g/	good, got, engaged
2 /dʒ/	message, engaged
3 /ŋ/	wrong, speaking, hang

Make sure you can say these three sounds clearly.

There are no rules, but there are some patterns.

g + a / o / u	/g/
g + consonant	/g/
g + e	/dʒ/
g + i	/g/ or /dʒ/
n + g	/ŋ/

There are exceptions, of course.
Example: *forget*
Check in a dictionary if you are not sure.
Remember: *g* can also be silent.
Examples: *through, sign*

Lesson 4: Applying new skills

A Each word below has two common meanings. Sometimes they are related. Sometimes they are different. What are the meanings in each case?
1. answer (noun and verb)
2. message (two nouns)
3. ring (noun and verb)
4. line (two nouns)
5. free (two adjectives)
6. hold (two verbs)
7. engaged (two adjectives)
8. call (two verbs)

B You are going to hear several telephone conversations.
1. Listen once straight through. Who does Gurkan talk to? Make a list.
2. Listen to Conversation 1 again. Say the next word in each pause.
3. Listen to Conversation 2 again. Complete Gurkan's sentences in each pause.
4. Listen to Conversation 3 again. Take Gurkan's message on the first form.

C Imagine you are the general manager's secretary. He calls you and asks if there are any messages. What do you say?

D Work in pairs. You are going to have two telephone conversations.

Conversation 1
Student A
Complete Message 1. Call B and give the information on the message.
Student B
Complete the blank form.

Conversation 2
Student B
Complete Message 2. Call A and give the information on the message.
Student A
Complete the blank form.

Phone Call

For _____
Date _____ Time _____ A.M. ☐ P.M. ☐
M _____ of _____
Tel. No. _____ ☐ Please call
Mob. No. _____ ☐ Will call again
Message _____

Urgent? _____ Signed _____

Message 1

Phone Call

For _____
Date _____ Time _____ A.M. ☐ P.M. ☐
M _____ of _____
Tel. No. _____ ☐ Please call
Mob. No. _____ ☐ Will call again
Message _____

Urgent? _____ Signed _____

Message 2

Phone Call

For _____
Date _____ Time _____ A.M. ☐ P.M. ☐
M _____ of _____
Tel. No. _____ ☐ Please call
Mob. No. _____ ☐ Will call again
Message _____

Urgent? _____ Signed _____

THEME 8 | Art and Literature | Joha and His Neighbour

In this theme you are going to tell some traditional stories.

Lesson 1: Vocabulary

You are going to learn some of the vocabulary you will need to tell the stories.

A Discuss these questions. They use some of the red words.
1. Who are the most famous *characters* from the *folklore* of your culture?
2. Who is your favourite character from *literature*? Why do you like him / her?
3. When you are with a group of friends, are you usually a *story-teller* or a *listener*?
4. Would you like to be a *writer*? If so, what sort of things would you like to write? If not, why not?

B Find and circle the regular verbs in the list of green words.
1. How do you say the past tense?
2. Read Skills Check 1. Can you see any patterns?
3. Practise saying the regular verbs.
4. Ask about the meaning of any new words.
5. Make a good sentence with each regular verb.

C Find and underline the irregular verbs in the list of green words.
1. What is the past tense?
2. Read Skills Check 2 and check.
3. Practise saying the regular verbs.
4. Ask about the meaning of any new words.
5. Make a good sentence with each regular verb.

D Cover the Skills Checks. Work in pairs. Test each other on the past tenses of the green words.

Skills Check 1

Saying past tense verbs – regular

Stories have many verbs in the past simple. Some are regular. The past simple of regular verbs ends in *ed*. The ending can be pronounced in three ways:

infinitive	past tense	ending
knock	knocked	= /t/
look	looked	
realise	realised	= /d/
borrow	borrowed	
hand	handed	= /ɪd/
wait	waited	

Skills Check 2

Saying past tense verbs – irregular

You must learn the form of irregular past tense verbs.
Examples:

infinitive	past
think	thought
see	saw
fall	fell
hear	heard

Irregular verbs ending in *t* often have the same form for the past tense.
Examples:

infinitive	past
put	put
hit	hit
cut	cut
hurt	hurt

character (n)

folklore (n)

listener (n)

literature (n)

story-teller (n)

writer (n)

borrow (v)

cut (v)

fall (v)

hand (give to) (v)

hear (v)

hurt (v)

knock (v)

lie (not tell truth) (v)

look (appear) (v)

realise (v)

return (give back) (v)

see (v)

think (v)

wait (v)

Lesson 2: Speaking

A Look at the adjectives in the blue box.
1 Put the adjectives in a logical order.
2 Think of nouns to go with each adjective.

> big   huge   small   tiny

B Look at the words in the yellow box.
1 Copy the words into the green table according to the stress pattern.
2 Use your dictionary to check stress and meaning.

> afternoon   angry   another   borrowed
> delighted   following   neighbour
> returned   sorry   surprised   visited

O o	o O	o o O	o O o	O o o

C Work in groups. You are going to put together a story called *Joha and the pots*.
1 Learn your piece of the story, then close your book.
2 Work with the other students to decide on the order of the pieces.
3 🎧 Listen and check your ideas.
4 Tell the whole story in order.
5 The ending is missing. How do you think the story ends?
6 Read the ending. It's at the bottom of page 38. Were you right?

a	"Could you give me my big pot back?" he said. "Certainly," said Joha. "Here you are." Joha handed the man his big pot and another small pot.
b	"I'd like my huge pot back, please," he said. "I'm sorry," said Joha. "Your pot died while I was using it."
c	"Please may I have my small pot back?" he said. "Of course," said Joha. "Here you are." Joha gave the man his small pot and another tiny one.
d	"What's this?" said the neighbour. "Your big pot had a baby while it was with me," said Joha.
e	"What's this?" said the other man. "Your small pot had a baby while it was in my house," said Joha.
f	A few days later, Joha borrowed a huge pot from his neighbour. He didn't bring it back the following day, so his neighbour visited him.
g	A few days later, Joha borrowed a big pot from his neighbour. He didn't take it back the following afternoon, so the man went to see him.
h	Joha borrowed a small pot from his neighbour. He didn't return the pot the next day, so his neighbour went round.
i	The neighbour was delighted and took his big pot and the small pot and went back to his house.
j	The neighbour was surprised, but he didn't say anything. He just took the small pot and the tiny pot and went home.

Lesson 3: Learning new skills

A Can you remember the story of *Joha and the pots*? Tell the story to each other in pairs.

B Here is the first part of the story from Lesson 2.
1. What is wrong with this version?
2. How can you improve it?
3. Read Skills Check 1 and check your ideas.
   Joha borrowed a small pot from his neighbour. Joha did not return the pot the next day, so his neighbour went round to see Joha, and his neighbour asked Joha for the pot.
   "Of course," said Joha. "Here you are."
   Joha gave his neighbour the small pot and another tiny pot.
   "Your pot had a baby while your pot was in my house," said Joha.

C Here is the middle of the story.
1. What is wrong with this version?
2. How can you improve it?
3. Read Skills Check 2 and check your ideas.
   A few days later, he borrowed a big pot from him. He did not return it the next day, so he went round to see him.
   "Please may I have it back?" he said.
   "Of course," he said. "Here you are." He gave it to him and another small one.

D Here is the end of the story.
1. What do the red words have in common?
2. Read Skills Check 3 and check your ideas.
3. Say the sentences with the correct pronunciation of the red words.
   A few days later, Joha borrowed *a* huge pot *from* his neighbour. He did not bring it back *the* next day, so his neighbour went round and asked *for* his pot.
   "I'm sorry," said Joha. "Your pot died while I *was* using it."
   The man *was* angry *and* said, "Pots don't die!"
   "They don't have babies either," said Joha, "but you *were* happy *to* take *the* other pots when you thought I *was* a fool."

Skills Check 1

Narrating a story (1) – Referring to people and things

We must **keep the interest of the listener**. Here are some ways:
1. Give the people names so that you can use the name sometimes.
2. Refer to people in other ways, e.g., *Joha's neighbour*.
3. Use *he / him, she / her* or *they / them* to refer to people.
4. Use *it / one* to refer to things.

Examples:
Joha borrowed a small pot from his neighbour, **Ali**. **He** did not return it, so the next day **Ali** went round to see **him** …
"Of course," said Joha. "Here you are." **He** gave **him** the pot and another tiny **one**.

Skills Check 2

Narrating a story (2) – Using names

Don't confuse the listener. Use the names of people regularly to make sure the listener doesn't get lost.

Examples:
A few days later, **Joha** borrowed a big pot from **Ali**. **He** did not return it the next day, so **Ali** went round to see **him**.
"Please may I have it back?" **he** said.
"Of course," **Joha** said. "Here you are." **He** gave the pot to **him** …

Skills Check 3

Saying unstressed words

A lot of words in an English sentence are not stressed. We say these with schwa /ə/.

Articles	a, an, the, some
Conjunctions	and, but
Parts of *be*	was / were
Some prepositions	for, from, to

SPEAKING SKILLS LEVEL 2 – THEME 8: Art and Literature, Joha and His Neighbour

Lesson 4: Applying new skills

A Read the sentences in the green box.
1 Underline the words with schwa /ə/.
2 Practise saying the sentences with the correct pronunciation.

a He had to see a man about some work.
b I went and got a book from the library for you to read.
c She was at a bus stop waiting for a bus.
d They were there at the start of the day.

B These words are in the stories below.

> afraid amazing believe continued evening future immediately other realised seconds tomorrow

1 Mark each stressed syllable.
2 Put a line (/) through syllables with /ə/.
3 Say the words with good pronunciation.

Skills Check

Reminder

Do you remember these sentences for narrators?

To introduce the story …	*Do you know the one about …?*
If you get lost …	*Now, where was I?*
If you leave something out …	*Oh, I forgot to say …*

C Work in pairs. You each have a Joha story.
1 Read your own story. Cover your partner's story.
2 Work in groups of people with the same story. Ask for help with any new words.
3 Work in pairs again. Close your book. Tell your partner your story. Remember the skills you learnt in Lesson 3 and the Skills Check Reminder on this page.
4 Listen to your partner's story. Tell your partner if you don't understand.

Joha and the donkey

One day, Ali, Joha's neighbour, came to Joha's house and asked to borrow his donkey for the day. "Of course," said Joha, and Ali took it away. Joha waited, but he didn't bring it back, so Joha went round to see him.
"Can I have my donkey back, please?" asked Joha.
"I'm sorry," said the man. "I'm afraid your donkey isn't here, but he'll be back tomorrow."
So Joha went round to his neighbour's house the following day and asked for the donkey again.
"I'm so sorry," said the other man. "My son took it to town, but he'll come back this evening."
Just then, Joha's donkey brayed in the neighbour's back garden! Joha was very angry.
"Neighbour! I'm surprised at you. You said my donkey isn't here, but I heard it bray in your back garden."
The other man looked angry.
"Joha. I'm surprised at you. How long have we known each other? Do you believe your neighbour or your donkey?"

Joha and the tree

One day, Joha was up a tree. He was cutting a branch to use on his fire. His neighbour, Ali, came out of his house and saw Joha in the tree. He realised immediately that Joha was cutting the branch that he was sitting on.
"Be careful, Joha," he said. "That branch will fall and you'll hurt yourself badly."
"I'm all right," said Joha, and continued cutting the branch, so Ali gave up and went back into his house. A few seconds later, Joha cut through the branch and it fell to the ground. Joha fell, too, into his neighbour's garden. He hurt himself badly. He lay on the ground, thinking.
"It is amazing," he thought. "My neighbour said the branch would fall and it fell. He said I'd hurt myself badly and I hurt myself badly."
He got up and ran to the back door of his neighbour's house. He knocked hard and the man came quickly.
"Wise neighbour," said Joha to Ali. "You can see the future. Tell me. When will I die?"

The man was angry. He said, "Pots don't die!" "They don't have babies either," said Joha, "but you were happy to take the other pots when you thought I was a fool."

THEME 9 Sports and Leisure — How Do You Play *Surakarta*?

In this theme you are going to talk about board games.

Lesson 1: Vocabulary

You are going to learn some vocabulary that you will need to talk about board games.

A Discuss these questions. They use the red words.
1. What sports can you play *indoors* or *outdoors*?
2. What sports do you play on a *court*?
3. The ball goes *out of court*. What happens next?
4. In which sports must you *hit* the ball over the *net*?
5. In which sports must you put the ball into the net?
6. What's the difference between a *player* and a *winner*?
7. How do you *serve* in tennis?
8. How many *points* must you *score* to win a game of tennis?

B 🎧 Read and listen to the text.
1. Find and label items in the picture with green words.
2. Explain the other green words.

F1 Racing

The game
F1 Racing is a game for two, three or four players, with all the fun of real car racing!

Contents
1 playing **board**, 4 playing **pieces** (1 red car, 1 blue car, 1 green car, 1 yellow car), 1 **spinner**

Object
You must get round the **track** faster than your **opponents**. Each race is 10 times round the track.

How to play
1. Each player must put his or her playing piece on the starting grid.
2. Each player **in turn** has a **go**. The player spins the spinner and moves the number of **squares**.
3. If a playing piece **lands on** the same square as an opponent's piece, that player must miss the next **turn**.
4. If a player gets a six, he or she can spin again.

C Discuss these questions.
1. Do you play board games?
2. What is your favourite board game?
3. How do you play it?

Red words:
court (n)
hit (n)
indoors (n)
net (n)
out of court (prep)
outdoors (n)
player (n)
point (n)
score (v)
serve (v)
winner (n)

Green words:
board (n)
go (n)
in turn (adv)
land on (v)
opponent (n)
piece (n)
spinner (n)
square (n)
track (n)
turn (n)

Lesson 2: Speaking

A Look at the playing board. Count the number of:
1 squares.
2 corners.
3 cross-points.
4 loops.

B Do you know this game? Can you guess how to play it?

C 🎧 Mino is talking to her friend, Munira. Listen to the first part of their conversation. Answer the questions.
1 What is special about today for Munira?
2 What are the arrangements for today?

D 🎧 Munira is opening her present from Mino. Listen to the second part of the conversation and complete the first section of the information leaflet – *The game*.

E 🎧 Listen to the third part.
1 Complete the rest of the leaflet.
2 Did you guess any of the details of the game correctly?

F Read the questions in the green box.
1 Find answers on the leaflet.
2 🎧 Listen again and check your ideas.

> a How many pieces does each player have?
> b How do you win the game?
> c Where must you put your counters at the beginning of the game?
> d How many counters can you move at each turn?
> e How many spaces can you move in each turn?
> f Can you move diagonally?
> g How can you take an opponent's piece?

G Work in pairs. Ask and answer the questions in the green box.

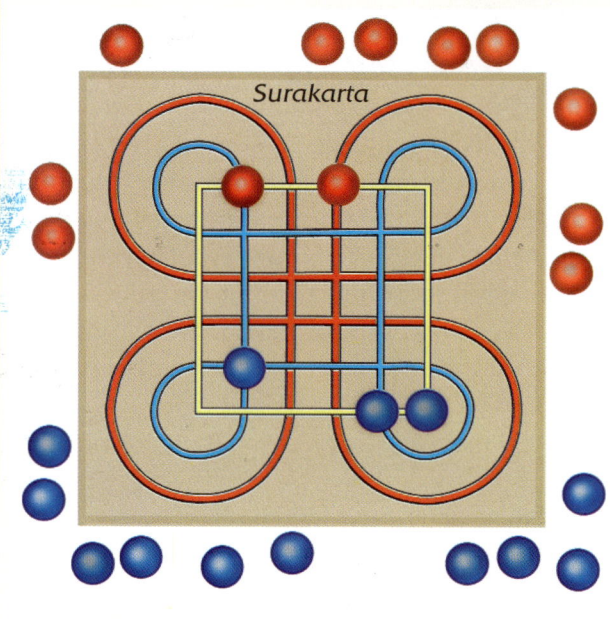

The game

_____ is a very old board game for two players. It takes its name from a town on the Indonesian island of _____.

Contents
1 playing _____, 24 _____ (12 red, 12 blue).

Object
You must take all your opponent's _____.

How to play
1 Each player must place his or her counters on the first two _____ of his or her side of the board. Each counter must be on a _____ or cross-point, i.e., **L** or **+**
2 Players take _____ to move one of their counters.
3 A counter can move one space.
4 A counter can move _____, _____ or diagonally.
5 A counter cannot _____ over another counter.
6 A counter cannot _____ on an occupied space (but see Rule 7).
7 You can take an opponent's piece by moving along a _____ of unoccupied spaces, but you must go round at least one _____.
8 Your opponent must take the counter off the board.

Lesson 3: Learning new skills

A Read the words lettered *a* to *l*. They are all in the conversation in Lesson 2.
1. What is special about all the words?
2. Read Skills Check 1 and check.
3. Match each word with a word numbered *1* to *12* with the same pronunciation.

a	board	1	ate	g	one	7	blew
b	blue	2	here	h	red	8	for
c	eight	3	bored	i	rows	9	too
d	four	4	read (past tense)	j	right	10	write
e	hear	5	rose	k	two	11	you're
f	know	6	no	l	your	12	won

B Read this part of the conversation from Lesson 2.
1. Write one word in each space. You can use the same word more than once.
2. Read Skills Check 2 and check.
3. How do you say *can* and *can't* in this conversation? Read Skills Check 3.
4. Practise the conversation in pairs. Be careful with the pronunciation of *do, must, can* and *can't*.

Mi: How _____ I win the game?
Mu: You _____ take all my pieces.
Mi: I see. How _____ we start?
Mu: Right. First rule. Each player _____ place the 12 counters on the first two rows of his or her side of the board.
Mi: I don't understand.
Mu: Each counter _____ be on a corner or cross-point.
Mi: Oh, I see. OK. I understand now.
Mu: Second rule. Players take turns to move one of their counters.
Mi: How many spaces _____ I move?
Mu: One space.
Mi: _____ I move backwards?
Mu: Yes, you _____. Forwards, backwards or diagonally.
Mi: What happens if there is another counter on that space? _____ I jump over a counter or take it?
Mu: No, you _____ jump over it and you _____ land on an occupied space.
Mi: So how _____ I take your pieces?
Mu: You _____ move along a line of unoccupied spaces, but you _____ go round at least one loop.

C Cover everything except the picture of the *Surakarta* playing board in Lesson 2. Mark playing pieces at the start of the game. Explain to each other the basic rules.

Skills Check 1
Homophones
Sometimes, two or more words in English have the same pronunciation.
Examples:
their / there / they're
too / two / to (when it is stressed)
Do not try to make any difference in the pronunciation. The listener will understand which word you mean from the context.

Skills Check 2
Explaining rules
We explain rules with *must, can* and *can't*.
Examples:

Giving the objective	You **must** take all your opponent's pieces to win.
Saying what is allowed	A counter **can** move one space.
Saying what is not allowed	You **can't** jump over a counter.

Skills Check 3
can and *can't*
When we write *can* or *can't*, it is easy to see the difference between the positive and the negative. But when we say *can't*, it is often difficult for the listener to hear the *nt* ending. For this reason, the negative has a different vowel sound in British English.

can	= /kən/*
can't	= /kɑːnt/

*except at the end of a sentence
Example: *Yes, you can.* = /kæn/

Lesson 4: Applying new skills

A Read each word in the yellow box. Think of another word with the same pronunciation but a different meaning and spelling.

> buy   flower   hole   I   mail   meat   piece   poor
> see   son   wait   way   week   where

B Work in groups. Discuss these questions.
1. What must you do every day / week / month to help your family?
2. What can you do *now* that you couldn't do a few years ago?
3. What can't you do because of the rules of your country / college / family?

> *I must do the shopping for my mother every day.*

> *I can stay out until 9.00 p.m. now.*

> *I can't drive. I'm too young.*

C Work in pairs. You each have the rules of a game.
1. Read the rules of your game. Cover your partner's rules.
2. Work in groups of people with the same game. Ask for help with any new words.
3. Work in pairs again. Close your book. Tell your partner the rules of your game. Answer his / her questions. Listen to your partner's game and ask questions.

LUDO

This is a game for 2, 3 or 4 players.

CONTENTS
1 playing board, 1 spinner, 16 counters (4 red, 4 green, 4 blue, 4 yellow)

OBJECT
You must get all your counters around the track and into the HOME area.

HOW TO PLAY
1. Each player places his or her counters in the starting circles of the same colour.
2. Players take turns to spin the spinner.
3. You must get a 6 before you can move a counter onto the track.
4. You can move any one counter the number of squares on the spinner.
5. If you get a 6, you get another go.
6. If a counter lands on the same square as an opponent's counter, you knock it off and it must return to the start.
7. If a counter lands on the same square as another one of your own counters, it makes a block. Your opponents' counters cannot pass a block.
8. When you get a counter all the way round the board, it can enter the HOME.
9. You must get the exact number to land in the HOME triangle. If you get more than the correct number of squares, you must go into HOME and back out again.

SNAKES AND LADDERS

This is a game for 2 players.

CONTENTS
1 playing board, 1 spinner, 2 counters (1 red, 1 blue)

OBJECT
You must get your counter into the HOME area before your opponent.

HOW TO PLAY
1. Each player places his or her counter in the starting area.
2. Players take turns to spin the spinner.
3. You must get a 6 before you can move a counter onto the track.
4. You must move your counter the number of squares on the spinner.
5. If you get a 6, you get another go.
6. If your counter lands on the same square as your opponent's counter, you must remove it and return it to the start.
7. If your counter lands on the bottom of a ladder, you must go up the ladder.
8. If your counter lands on the head of a snake, you must go down the snake.
9. You must get the exact number to land in the HOME area. If you get more than the correct number of squares, you must go into HOME and back out again.

THEME 10 Nutrition and Health Truths and Myths

In this theme you are going to talk about some truths and some myths about health.

Lesson 1: Vocabulary

You are going to learn some vocabulary that you will need to talk about the truths and the myths.

A How can you make a sandwich? Use some of the red words in your answer.

B Read the list of words in the blue box.
Which word in the list connects them all?
1 Say each word aloud.
2 Match the word to the sound of the (stressed) vowel.
3 Think of another word with each vowel sound.
4 Test each other on the vowel sounds in pairs.

hand	/ɑː/
leg	/æ/
body	/e/
skin	/ɪ/
teeth	/iː/
tooth	/ɒ/
arm	/ʊ/
foot	/uː/

add (v)
cut (v)
gram (n)
pepper (n)
piece (n)
put on (v)
tomato (n)
arm (n)
body (n)
ear (n)
eye (n)
face (n)
foot (n)
hair (n)
hand (n)
leg (n)
mouth (n)
nose (n)
skin (n)
teeth (n)
tooth (n)

C Look at the drawing (Figure 1).
1 What does it show?
2 What does each symbol mean?
3 What is the connection between all the sounds?
4 Think of another word with each diphthong.
5 Test each other on the diphthongs in pairs.

Figure 1: /ə bɔɪz feɪs/

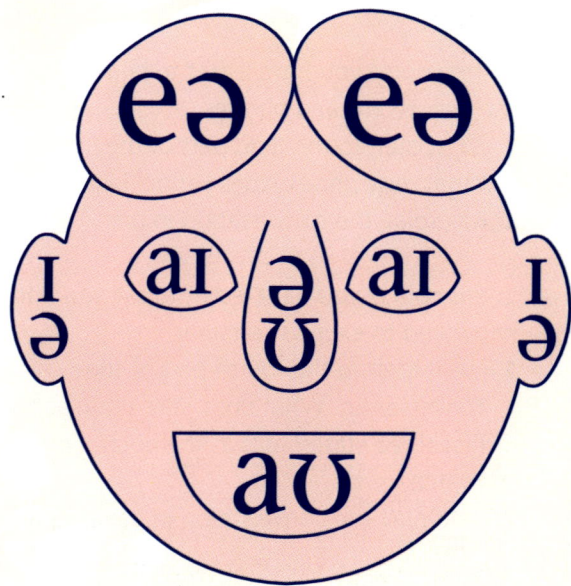

D Discuss these questions. They use some of the green words.
1 Have you ever broken …
 • your *arm*?
 • your *leg*?
2 How do you look after …
 • your *eyes*?
 • your *teeth*?
 • your *hair*?
 • your *skin*?
3 How can you deal with …
 • a *nose*bleed?
 • a *head*ache?
 • a *tooth*ache?
4 In what ways are your *hand* and your *foot* similar?
 (There are at least three ways.)

Lesson 2: Speaking review (1)

A Look at the quiz.
1 What is it about?
2 What do you have to do?

B In this course you have learnt to ask about feelings.
1 Complete the sentences in the conversation with a suitable word in each space.
2 🎧 Listen to the first part of the conversation and check your ideas.
   V: Hi, Fatima. How are you?
   F: I'm OK.
   V: What's the _____?
   F: _____, really.
   V: Come _____. Tell me what's _____.

C 🎧 In this course you have learnt to talk about arrangements. Listen to the second part of the conversation. What arrangements does Fatima talk about? Use these words.

| parents   relatives   brother |

D In this course you have learnt to talk about information you have heard.
1 How does Fatima show that she has heard the information about Munira's arrangements?
2 🎧 Listen to the second part of the conversation again and check.

E In this course you have learnt to hear, check and use new words and phrases.
1 🎧 Listen to the third part of the conversation. What new phrase does Fatima learn?
2 Role-play the conversation in pairs.

F In this course you have learnt to say you don't know and to express certainty.
1 🎧 Listen to the fourth part of the conversation. What does Vera think about the first three statements in the quiz? What about Fatima?
2 Role-play the conversation in pairs.

G Do the rest of the quiz in pairs.

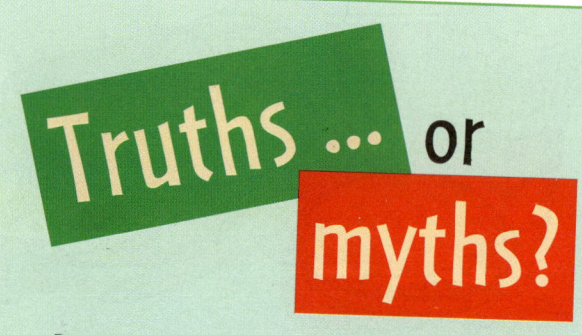

Truths ... or myths?

Read each statement about hair, eyes, skin and teeth. Is it true or false? Decide, then turn to page 45 to find the facts!

A Your hair

	Me	You
1 Washing damages your hair. You should not wash your hair more than once a week.		
2 If you cut your hair, it will grow faster.		
3 You can repair split ends with the right shampoo.		
4 Brushing is good for your hair. You should brush your hair at least 40 times a day.		

B Your eyes

1 Eating carrots will improve your eyesight.		
2 If you sit too close to the television, you can damage your eyes.		
3 Cucumbers are good for your eyes.		
4 If you don't get enough sleep, you will get dark circles under your eyes.		

C Your skin

1 If you eat fatty foods like chips, you will get oily skin.		
2 Stress causes spots.		
3 Make-up causes spots.		
4 You can get rid of spots by washing more often.		

D Your teeth

1 Cleaning your teeth with your finger is better than cleaning them with a toothbrush.		
2 If your gums bleed, stop brushing your teeth in that area.		
3 If you keep an aspirin tablet beside a painful tooth, it will reduce the toothache.		
4 A hard toothbrush is better than a soft one.		

Lesson 3: Speaking review (2)

A Read the piece(s) of information (below) that the teacher asks you to read. Learn the information. Practise saying it aloud with good pronunciation – see the Skills Check Reminder.

B Your teacher is going to read out the statements from the quiz (Lesson 2). Does your information prove or disprove the statement? If it does, say (don't read!) your information.

> **Skills Check**
>
> **Reminder**
>
> In this course you have learnt to:
> - say words with the correct stress.
> - say the schwa /ə/ sound correctly.
> - say consonant clusters correctly.
> - say function words (*a, an, the*, etc.) correctly.
> - say *can* and *can't* correctly.

C Work in pairs. Match each statement in the quiz (Lesson 2) with one piece of information below.
1 Does the information say the statement is true or false?
2 Do you agree with the information? Why (not)?
3 Do some research to check statements you are not sure about.

1 A toothbrush with bristles is much better at cleaning food from your teeth than a finger. Your finger cannot reach all the areas as well as a brush does.

2 Bleeding is a sign that gums are not healthy. It usually means you have small pieces of food stuck around your teeth. If you don't remove the food, your gums will continue to bleed. Brush your teeth with a soft toothbrush. The bleeding will gradually reduce and disappear.

3 Brushing is very, very bad for your hair. It is one of the main reasons for split ends. Brush your hair to make it tidy, but stop then.

4 Carrots are rich in vitamin A, which helps to keep the retinas of the eyes healthy. However, carrots can't improve your vision. In fact, eating large amounts of vitamin A can be very harmful.

5 Cutting your hair only makes it shorter. Hair grows almost exactly 1 cm per month, whether you cut it or not.

6 Dark circles under the eyes are often the result of a vitamin B deficiency caused by stress or poor diet, but lack of sleep can also cause them.

7 If the skin around your eyes is red, cucumber can help, but don't eat it. Put slices on your eyes for 10 or 15 minutes.

8 Sitting too close to the television does not damage your eyes. However, if you have to sit close to the television to see clearly, maybe you should get an eye test anyway.

9 Skin is naturally oily or dry or a combination. You do not get oily skin from fatty food.

10 Make-up can fill up your pores and cause spots. Buy "nonacnegenic" products – they won't fill up your pores.

11 Normal everyday stress doesn't cause spots. Very high stress, from the death of a relative for example, can result in your skin producing more oil, but that still doesn't mean you'll get more spots.

12 Washing does not damage hair, but the shampoo you use might damage it.

13 Hard bristles on a toothbrush can damage the gums. Soft bristles can get into small spaces between teeth and clean better.

14 Washing your face cannot remove spots, but it can help to remove the dead skin that fills up pores and causes spots. Wash your face twice a day with a mild soap. After washing, gently dry your skin with a soft towel.

15 You cannot repair split ends with any shampoo. You should cut hair with split ends immediately or your hair will split higher and look even worse.

16 You cannot stop toothache by putting an aspirin tablet anywhere in the mouth. In fact, it is dangerous to do this because aspirin burns the soft tissues of the mouth. Take the aspirin after eating some food. It will help with the pain, but go to see a dentist as soon as possible.

Lesson 4: Speaking review (3)

A In this course you have learnt a lot of new words. Play noughts and crosses. Use one of the words in a good sentence with good pronunciation.

kinaesthetic	argument	concentration
process	temperature	ceremony
extension	realise	opponent

B In this course you have given several talks. Choose one of these subjects from the course. Find your notes or write the talk again. Give your talk in small groups.

Theme 3	The Time Thieves
Theme 4	Natural Cycles
Theme 5	My Country and Another Country
Theme 6	Wedding Customs in My Country
Theme 9	A Board Game in My Culture

C In this course you have learnt to make a lot of statements and to reply correctly.
  1 Read the phrases on the left. Complete each phrase with a suitable word.
  2 Find a good reply in each case.
  3 Practise the statements and replies in pairs.

  a What's the _____?
  b I'm sorry. I won't do it _____.
  c Are you _____ next week?
  d I can't _____ it at three o'clock.
  e Where _____ we meet?
  f I _____ see you at three o'clock on Monday in the cafe.
  g What's the population of your _____?
  h Rainfall is _____ in my country than in your country.
  i I'm _____ married next weekend.
  j I _____ there are bridesmaids at British weddings.
  k Can you _____ the line?
  l Can I _____ a message?
  m Can I _____ diagonally?

  1 How about the Garden Mall?
  2 I have no idea.
  3 No, it's OK. I'll call back.
  4 No, only forwards and backwards.
  5 No, sorry. I'm busy.
  6 Nothing.
  7 OK. Forget it.
  8 OK. I'll look forward to it.
  9 Really? Congratulations!
  10 Really? What are they?
  11 Really? What's the average, then?
  12 What about four, then?
  13 Yes, certainly.

D In this course you have learnt to give advice. Work in pairs.
  1 Choose one of the statements in the quiz in Lesson 2. Find the matching piece of information in Lesson 3.
  2 Write a short conversation. One person has read the statement from the quiz somewhere. The other person knows the information from Lesson 3.

  Examples:
  A: I understand that washing damages your hair.
  B: Where did you hear that?
  A: I don't know. But apparently, you shouldn't wash your hair more than once a week.
  B: That's not true, actually. Washing doesn't damage hair.
  A: Really?
  B: No, it doesn't. But the shampoo you use might damage it.

  B: I read that cucumber is good for your eyes.
  A: Yes, that's true.
  B: So I'm going to eat cucumber sandwiches every day.
  A: No, you don't eat the cucumber. You put it on your eyes.
  B: Really?
  A: Yes. Put it on your eyes for 10 or 15 minutes if the skin around your eyes is red.

Word Lists: Thematic

THEME 1
Education, What Kind of a Learner Are You?

- college (n)
- meeting (n)
- speech (n)
- studies (n)
- subject (n)
- year (n)
- aural (adj)
- kinaesthetic (adj)
- learner (n)
- mode (n)
- visual (adj)

THEME 2
Daily Life, I'm Sorry

- breakfast (n)
- diary (n)
- dinner (n)
- last (v)
- period (n)
- second (n)
- angry (adj)
- apologise (v)
- argue (v)
- argument (n)
- calm (adj)
- deal with (v)
- matter (n and v)
- sorry (adj)
- upset (adj)
- wrong (adj)

THEME 3
Work and Business, The Time Thieves

- assistant (n)
- checkout (n)
- clerk (n)
- counsellor (n)
- guide (n)
- operator (n)
- telesales (n)
- colleague (n)
- concentrate (v)
- concentration (n)
- distract (v)
- organise (v)
- TO DO list (n)
- urgent (adj)

THEME 4
Science and Nature, Natural Cycles

- diagram (n)
- experiment (n)
- explain (v)
- explanation (n)
- natural (adj)
- sunrise (n)
- sunset (n)
- animal (n)
- carbon (n)
- convert (v)
- cycle (n)
- gas (n)
- hydrogen (n)
- liquid (n)
- nitrogen (n)
- oxygen (n)
- plant (n)
- process (n)
- solid (n)

THEME 5
The Physical World, Do You Know Your Country?

Africa (n)

America (n)

Asia (n)

continent (n)

Europe (n)

Oceania (n)

the Middle East (n)

area (n)

climate (n)

location (n)

population (n)

region (n)

temperature (n)

THEME 6
Culture and Civilization, Good Luck!

birth (n)

culture (n)

luck (n)

lucky (adj)

relative (n)

special (adj)

star sign (n)

bride (n)

ceremony (n)

get married (v)

groom (n)

marriage (n)

wedding (n)

THEME 7
They Made Our World, Can You Speak Telephone?

captain (n)

cyclist (n)

helicopter (n)

invent (v)

invention (n)

inventor (n)

ride (v)

rider (n)

answer (the phone) (v)

call (v)

dial (v)

engaged (adj)

extension (n)

free (adj)

hang up (v)

hold (the line) (v)

pick up (v)

put through (v)

switchboard (n)

telephonist (n)

tone (n)

THEME 8
Art and Literature, Joha and His Neighbour

character (n)

folklore (n)

listener (n)

literature (n)

story-teller (n)

writer (n)

borrow (v)

cut (v)

fall (v)

hand (give to) (v)

hear (v)

hurt (v)

knock (v)

lie (not tell truth) (v)

look (appear) (v)

realise (v)

return (give back) (v)

see (v)

think (v)

wait (v)

Word Lists: Alphabetical

THEME 9
Sports and Leisure, How Do You Play *Surakarta?*

- court (n)
- hit (n)
- indoors (n)
- net (n)
- out of court (prep)
- outdoors (n)
- player (n)
- point (n)
- score (v)
- serve (v)
- winner (n)
- board (n)
- go (n)
- in turns (adv)
- land on (v)
- opponent (n)
- piece (n)
- spinner (n)
- square (n)
- track (n)
- turn (n)

THEME 10
Nutrition and Health, Truths and Myths

- add (v)
- cut (v)
- gram (n)
- pepper (n)
- piece (n)
- put on (v)
- tomato (n)
- arm (n)
- body (n)
- ear (n)
- eye (n)
- face (n)
- foot (n)
- hair (n)
- hand (n)
- leg (n)
- mouth (n)
- nose (n)
- skin (n)
- teeth (n)
- tooth (n)

- add (v)
- Africa (n)
- America (n)
- angry (adj)
- animal (n)
- answer (the phone) (v)
- apologise (v)
- area (n)
- argue (v)
- argument (n)
- arm (n)
- Asia (n)
- assistant (n)
- aural (adj)
- birth (n)
- board (n)
- body (n)
- borrow (v)
- breakfast (n)
- bride (n)
- call (v)
- calm (adj)
- captain (n)
- carbon (n)
- ceremony (n)
- character (n)
- checkout (n)
- clerk (n)
- climate (n)
- colleague (n)
- college (n)
- concentrate (v)
- concentration (n)
- continent (n)
- convert (v)
- counsellor (n)
- court (n)
- culture (n)
- cut (v)
- cut (v)
- cycle (n)
- cyclist (n)
- deal with (v)
- diagram (n)
- dial (v)
- diary (n)
- dinner (n)
- distract (v)
- ear (n)
- engaged (adj)
- Europe (n)
- experiment (n)
- explain (v)
- explanation (n)
- extension (n)
- eye (n)
- face (n)

SPEAKING SKILLS LEVEL 2

fall (v)	last (v)	period (n)	star sign (n)
folklore (n)	learner (n)	pick up (v)	story-teller (n)
foot (n)	leg (n)	piece (n)	studies (n)
free (adj)	lie (not tell truth) (v)	piece (n)	subject (n)
gas (n)	liquid (n)	plant (n)	sunrise (n)
get married (v)	listener (n)	player (n)	sunset (n)
go (n)	literature (n)	point (n)	switchboard (n)
gram (n)	location (n)	population (n)	teeth (n)
groom (n)	look (appear) (v)	process (n)	telephonist (n)
guide (n)	luck (n)	put on (v)	telesales (n)
hair (n)	lucky (adj)	put through (v)	temperature (n)
hand (give to) (v)	marriage (n)	realise (v)	the Middle East (n)
hand (n)	matter (n and v)	region (n)	think (v)
hang up (v)	meeting (n)	relative (n)	TO DO list (n)
hear (v)	mode (n)	return (give back) (v)	tomato (n)
helicopter (n)	mouth (n)	ride (v)	tone (n)
hit (n)	natural (adj)	rider (n)	tooth (n)
hold (the line) (v)	net (n)	score (v)	track (n)
hurt (v)	nitrogen (n)	second (n)	turn (n)
hydrogen (n)	nose (n)	see (v)	upset (adj)
in turn (adv)	Oceania (n)	serve (v)	urgent (adj)
indoors (n)	operator (n)	skin (n)	visual (adj)
invent (v)	opponent (n)	solid (n)	wait (v)
invention (n)	organise (v)	sorry (adj)	wedding (n)
inventor (n)	out of court (prep)	special (adj)	winner (n)
kinaesthetic (adj)	outdoors (n)	speech (n)	writer (n)
knock (v)	oxygen (n)	spinner (n)	wrong (adj)
land on (v)	pepper (n)	square (n)	year (n)

Tapescript

Presenter: **Skills in English**
Speaking: Level 2
Theme 1: Education, What Kind of a Learner Are You?
Lesson 1: Vocabulary
D Read and listen to the text. Complete it with a green word in each space.

Voice: How do you learn? If you like pictures, graphs and charts, you are probably a visual learner. Visual means *of the eyes*. If you like talking about new information with your friends, you are probably an aural learner. Aural means *of the ears*.
If you like using the library and the Internet to find new information, you are probably a read / write learner. In other words, you need to read things or write them to remember them.
If you always like to do things with your hands, you are probably a kinaesthetic learner. Kinaesthetic means *of feeling and movement*.
If you like to do two or more of these things, you are probably a multi-mode learner. Mode means *method* or *way of doing something*, and multi means many.

Presenter: **Lesson 3:** Checking skills
A 1 Listen to each pair of words.

Voice:
a	arm	am
b	read	rid
c	work	walk
d	main	mine
e	learn	lean
f	now	no
g	car	can't
h	wear	we're
i	try	tray
j	more	mall
k	she's	cheese
l	break	brick
m	like	lake
n	police	please
o	mode	made

Presenter: **Lesson 4:** Applying skills
A 2 Listen to two girls doing the questionnaire.

Anna: OK. First question. Your friend asks you for directions to your house. Would you (a) draw a map; (b) tell him or her … Sorry, how do you say this word: D-I-R-E-C-T-I-O-N-S?
Maria: Directions.
Anna: Right. Would you (b) tell him or her the directions; (c) write down the directions (without a map); or (d) offer to collect him or her?
Maria: What does *collect* mean?
Anna: It means go and bring her to your house.
Maria: Let me think. I would draw a map and tell her the directions.
Anna: OK. So that's *a* and *b*.

Presenter: **Theme 2: Daily Life, I'm Sorry**
Lesson 1: Vocabulary
B 2 Listen and check your answers.

Voice: Sorry – the best word in the world.
Do you ever have arguments with your friends? What do you usually argue about? Research by this magazine shows that most arguments between young children are about possessions.
That's my pen.
No, it isn't. It's mine.

But as children get older, the cause of arguments changes. Most arguments between teenagers are about words or feelings.
You said I was stupid!
No, I didn't.
Yes, you did. You told Fernando Vasquez that I was stupid and childish.
It is natural to be upset by an argument, but you should try not to get angry. If you stay calm, it is much easier to deal with the problem. Ask your friend:
What's wrong?
or
What's the matter?
Once you know the cause, apologise – even if you didn't mean to do it. Just say, 'I'm sorry.' It is very hard to stay angry with someone who apologises.

Presenter: D 2 Listen and check your answers.
Voice: breakfast
diary
dinner
period
second
angry
apologise
argue
argument
matter
sorry
upset

Presenter: **Lesson 2:** Speaking
B Vera's friend, Phyllis, comes into the cafe. Listen to the conversation. Which of the actions in Exercise A does Vera choose?
Phyllis: Morning, Vera. How are you?
Vera: Fine.
Phyllis: What's wrong?
Vera: Nothing.
Phyllis: Come on. Tell me. What's the matter?
Vera: I told you. Nothing.
Phyllis: There is something. Are you angry with me?
Vera: No.
Phyllis: Yes, you are.
Vera: I said I'm not.
Phyllis: Tell me what's wrong.
Vera: Just forget it.
Phyllis: OK.

Presenter: C 2 Listen again and check your ideas.
[REPEAT OF LESSON 2 EXERCISE B]

Presenter: E Listen to another conversation between Vera and Phyllis.
Phyllis: Morning, Vera. How are you?
Vera: Fine.
Phyllis: What's wrong?
Vera: I'm upset.
Phyllis: Why are you upset?
Vera: You made fun of me.

Phyllis:	No, I didn't.		A:	OK. I forgive you.
Vera:	Yes, you did. You said I was stupid.		B:	Thanks.
Phyllis:	When?			
Vera:	Just now. In front of my parents.		Presenter:	**Theme 3: Work and Business, The Time Thieves**
Phyllis:	Did I? I'm sorry. I didn't mean it.			**Lesson 1:** Vocabulary
Vera:	It upset me.			D Listen to a short talk about working on your own. Then complete the text with a green word or phrase in each space. Make any necessary changes.
Phyllis:	I'm really sorry. It was a silly thing to say.			
Vera:	But you think I'm stupid.			
Phyllis:	I don't really. Look, I'm really, really sorry. I won't do it again.		Male voice:	Do you find it difficult to concentrate when you are working on your own? Can you just sit down and start work, or do little things distract you all the time? I don't have a problem when it is something I enjoy – a good film or a good book, for example. But as soon as I try to do some work, something, or someone, comes along and distracts me. My mobile phone rings, or a colleague from college comes by for a chat. I try to organize my time. I make a TO DO list most days. It is usually very long, because I didn't do all the things yesterday or the day before. I sit down at my desk, and immediately I feel hungry or thirsty, or I suddenly think of something urgent that I have to do. I must learn to concentrate when I am working on my own. What can I do to improve my concentration?
Vera:	That's OK. I forgive you!			

Presenter: **F** Listen again to Phyllis's sentences in the second conversation. What does Vera reply in each case?

Phyllis: Morning, Vera. How are you?
What's wrong?
Why are you upset?
No, I didn't.
When?
Did I? I'm sorry. I didn't mean it.
I'm really sorry. It was a silly thing to say.
I don't really. Look, I'm really, really sorry. I won't do it again.

Presenter: **Lesson 3:** Learning new skills
A 3 Listen and check your ideas.

A:	What's wrong?
B:	It's nothing.
A:	What's the matter?
B:	It's not important.
A:	Are you angry with me?
B:	No. Just forget it.
A:	You have to tell me what's wrong.
B:	OK. You were rude to me.
A:	I'm sorry. I didn't mean to be rude.
B:	You said I was stupid.
A:	I'm really sorry. It was a silly thing to say.
B:	I'm not stupid.
A:	I know. I won't say it again.

Presenter: **Lesson 4:** Applying new skills
A 1 Listen and check your ideas.

Voice:
anyone	column 1
assignment	column 2
concentrate	column 1
decision	column 2
hard-working	column 2
organise	column 1
serious	column 1
solution	column 2
studying	column 1
untidy	column 2

Presenter: B 2 Listen and check your ideas.
Voice:
between
distract
friendly
hungry
idea
lecture
mobile
problem
study
tired
upset

Presenter: B 2 Listen and check your ideas.
Voice:
a The conversation is between Vera Ferry and her friend, Phyllis, in the cafe.
b Phyllis made fun of Vera.
c Telephone and get very angry.
d Visit and explain how you feel.
e You have to talk face to face about your feelings.

Presenter: **Lesson 4:** Applying new skills
D 2 Listen and check your ideas.

A:	Morning, how are you?
B:	Fine.
A:	What's wrong?
B:	Nothing.
A:	Come on. What's the matter?
B:	I told you. Nothing.
A:	Why are you upset?
B:	You made fun of me.
A:	You broke my pen!
B:	I'm sorry. I didn't mean to break it.
A:	Then you said it was a stupid pen anyway.
B:	I'm really sorry. It was a silly thing to say.
A:	Yes, it was. It upset me.
B:	I'm really, really sorry. I won't do it again.
A:	Will you get me a new pen?
B:	Of course.

Presenter: D Listen to the recorded talk. How could you improve your talk?

Female voice: I'm going to talk about how to deal with Time Thieves. Time Thieves distract you from your work. You must beat the Time Thieves so you can get on and do your work. I'm going to mention four problems. Firstly, the mobile phone. Does your mobile phone never stop ringing? Turn it off, or tell people not to call you at a certain time each day. They can call if it's an emergency, but not if they just want to chat.
Secondly, the hard-working colleague. She wants help with the latest assignment. This Time Thief is difficult, because you don't want to upset her. Tell her that you will help her later.
Thirdly, the untidy desk. Many people want to work in a tidy place. But remember. This time is for studying,

not tidying. Put everything in a drawer and get on with your work. You can tidy the drawer another time. Finally, the tired brain. Do you find you feel tired when you sit down to study? Choose a good time to study – don't try to study after a heavy meal. Have a light meal and take a glass of water to your study room. It is better than coffee to help you concentrate.
Those are my four problems and four solutions. Are you going to follow my advice?

Presenter: **Theme 4: Science and Nature, Natural Cycles**
Lesson 1: Vocabulary
B 2 Listen and check your answers.

Male voice: Three natural cycles keep the plants and animals on Earth alive. The cycles are the carbon and oxygen cycle; the nitrogen cycle; and the water cycle. All living things need oxygen (O), carbon (C), nitrogen (N) and water, which is, of course, a combination of hydrogen and oxygen (H_2O).
How does a natural cycle work? The process is simple. Something converts or changes the form of a substance. Something else converts it back again. For example, in the water cycle, the heat of the sun converts liquid water in rivers and seas into a gas. We see this gas in the sky as a white, grey or black cloud. Then, the gas cools and changes back to a liquid – called rain – or a solid – called snow.

Presenter: **Lesson 2:** Speaking
A Brenda Pride is calling her friend Trisha Crane on the phone. Listen to their conversation.

Brenda: Hi, Trisha. It's Brenda.
Trisha: Hello, Brenda. How are things?
Brenda: Fine. Well, actually, I need some help.
Trisha: Of course. What can I do for you?
Brenda: Are you free this afternoon?
Trisha: Yes, I think so. What time is good for you?
Brenda: What about two o'clock?
Trisha: No, sorry. I can't make it then. I've got a lecture until 3.00.
Brenda: OK. Can we meet at 3.15 in the college cafe?
Trisha: Yes, sure. I'll see you at quarter past three.
Brenda: Great. Thanks.
Trisha: What's it about?
Brenda: I'll tell you then.
Trisha: All right. Bye.

Presenter: **B 2 Listen again and check your answers.**
[REPEAT OF LESSON 2 EXERCISE A]

Presenter: **D Brenda and Trisha are meeting at the college. Listen to their conversation. Complete the information about Brenda's assignment.**

Trisha: So, what's wrong?
Brenda: I need some help with my assignment.
Trisha: What's it about?
Brenda: I have to describe a cycle.
Trisha: What do you mean? A bicycle?
Brenda: No! A *natural* cycle.
Trisha: Ah. Like the water cycle?
Brenda: Exactly. That's what I'm going to do. The water cycle. I think the other two are too hard.
Trisha: What are the other two?
Brenda: The nitrogen cycle and the, um, what is it … oh, yes, the carbon and oxygen cycle.
Trisha: So what's the problem?
Brenda: I have to give the talk to the group next week.
Trisha: Right.
Brenda: And I need someone to listen and see if it makes sense.
Trisha: Well, it won't make sense to me. I'm not in the Science Faculty.
Brenda: It will make sense – at least, it should make sense, because I have to explain any technical words in the talk.
Trisha: OK. I'm ready.
Brenda: No, it's a bit more complicated than that. I have to describe it and they have to draw it. So I want to see if you can draw it from my description.
Trisha: But I'm no good at drawing.
Brenda: Well, you can just write words in boxes and draw arrows if you like.
Trisha: Oh. OK.
Brenda: Right. Are you ready?
Trisha: Yes.

Presenter: **E Brenda is going to describe the water cycle. Listen and complete the diagram with suitable words in each box. Draw arrows to show movement from one box to the next.**

Brenda: OK. I'm going to describe the water cycle. Can you try to draw it? Firstly, water evaporates from the sea. Evaporates is spelt E-V-A-P-O-R-A-T-E-S. It means that the water changes from a liquid to a gas. The water vapour – that's V-A-P-O-U-R – or gas, rises into the air. Then, the water vapour condenses. That's C-O-N-D-E-N-S-E-S. It's the opposite of 'evaporates'. In other words, it changes from a gas to a liquid. It forms clouds. The clouds move over the land and they rise. They cool over hills and mountains. The cold air can't hold as much water, so storm clouds form and rain or snow falls onto the land. The rainwater runs into rivers. The rivers flow into the sea and the cycle starts all over again. OK. Show me your drawing.

Presenter: **Lesson 3:** Learning new skills
A 3 Listen and check.

A: Are you free next week?
B: Yes, I think so.
A: What day is good for you?
B: Can we meet on Wednesday?
A: No, sorry. I'm busy then.
B: What about Thursday?
A: Yes, sure.
B: What time is good for you?
A: Can we meet at 12.00?
B: Yes, that's fine.
A: Where shall we meet?
B: How about the main entrance?
A: OK. I'll see you on Thursday at 12.00 in the main entrance.
B: Great. What's it about?
A: I'll tell you then.
B: OK.

Presenter: **Theme 5: The Physical World, Do You Know Your Country?**
Lesson 1: Vocabulary
C Read and listen to the green words.

Voice: area
climate
location
population

region
temperature

Presenter: **Lesson 2:** Speaking
A 2 Listen and check your ideas.
Dave: Hi, Brad. How are you?
Brad: I'm fine.
Dave: Are you free for a coffee?
Brad: No, sorry. I have a lecture now.
Dave: What about later?
Brad: What time?
Dave: How about 11.00?
Brad: Yes, I can make that.
Dave: Shall we meet in the cafe?
Brad: Yes, sure. See you then.

Presenter: B Dave and Brad meet later. Listen to the conversation and answer the questions.
Dave: There you are. One black coffee with no sugar.
Brad: Thanks.
Dave: What's wrong?
Brad: It's nothing really.
Dave: Come on. Tell me. Are you angry with me?
Brad: No, of course not.
Dave: Are you worried about something?
Brad: Well … we've got a quiz in the next lesson.
Dave: That sounds like fun.
Brad: Yes, except … you have to answer questions about your own country.
Dave: What's wrong with that?
Brad: I don't know anything about my own country.
Dave: Don't be silly. I'm sure you know lots.
Brad: Go on, then. Ask me a question.
Dave: OK. What's the population? I mean, how many people are there?
Brad: I don't know.
Dave: Oh. OK. What's the area? How big is it?
Brad: I have no idea.
Dave: Oh dear. All right, here's an easy one. What's the average temperature in summer?
Brad: I'm not sure.
Dave: Oh, come on! What do you *think*?! You've lived there for years!
Brad: I think it's about 35.
Dave: There. You do know something.
Brad: Or it might be lower …
Dave: OK … so 33 or 34 …
Brad: Or it could be higher …
Dave: What!? Look, you should go to the library *now* and do some research.
Brad: I don't have time. The lesson's in 10 minutes.
Dave: That's OK. Log on. Go to google.com and look up your country on the Internet. Just type the name and … oh, I don't know … population. You will get all the facts easily.
Brad: Right. Thanks.
Dave: Don't thank me. Just go! Quickly!
Brad: What about my coffee?
Dave: I'll drink it.

Presenter: C Listen again to part of the conversation.
Dave: OK. What's the population? How many people are there?
Brad: I don't know.
Dave: Oh. OK. What's the area? I mean, how big is it?
Brad: I have no idea.
Dave: Oh dear. All right, here's an easy one. What's the average temperature in summer?
Brad: I'm not sure.

Presenter: D Listen again to the next part.
Dave: Oh, come on! What do you *think*?! You've lived there for years!
Brad: I think it's about 35.
Dave: There. You do know something.
Brad: Or it might be lower …
Dave: OK … so 33 or 34 …
Brad: Or it could be higher …
Dave: What!?

Presenter: **Theme 6: Culture and Civilization, Good Luck!**
Lesson 2: Speaking
A Gary and Sami are doing the same course at Greenhill College. Listen to the first part of their conversation.
Gary: What are you doing next weekend?
Sami: I'm getting married.
Gary: Sorry? What did you say?
Sami: I said I'm getting married.
Gary: Really? I don't believe it!
Sami: Why not?
Gary: Because I didn't know that you were engaged!

Presenter: B Listen to the whole conversation. How does Gary define each of these words?
Gary: What are you doing next weekend?
Sami: I'm getting married.
Gary: Sorry? What did you say?
Sami: I said I'm getting married.
Gary: Really? I don't believe it!
Sami: Why not?
Gary: Because I didn't know that you were engaged!
Sami: What do you mean, engaged?
Gary: Engaged means, I don't know how to explain. It's when you say you want to marry someone; you promise to marry someone.
Sami: Oh, I see.
Gary: In my culture, we exchange rings when we get engaged.
Sami: Exchange?
Gary: Yes, the man gives the woman a ring and the woman gives the man a ring. They are called engagement rings. Do you get engaged in your culture?
Sami: No, not really. Well, we agree to get married, of course, but we don't change …
Gary: *Ex*change.
Sami: Exchange rings.
Gary: Who is your fiancée?
Sami: My fiancée?
Gary: I mean, who are you engaged to?
Sami: My fiancée is called Dana. She's a student in the third year.
Gary: Right. Where are you going for the honeymoon?
Sami: The what?
Gary: The honeymoon. You know, that's the holiday after your wedding.
Sami: *What* is it called?
Gary: A honeymoon.
Sami: Like honey and moon?
Gary: Yes, exactly.
Sami: Why is it called a honeymoon?
Gary: Well, at one time a lot of couples ran away and stayed away for a month – a honey month – to give the bride's father time to get honeyed or sweet again.

	Nowadays, honeymoons are usually much shorter. But anyway, where are you going?	Voice:	If you call an organisation with a lot of telephones, your call will probably go to a switchboard. The telephonist will ask you for a name and put you through to that person's extension number. She will ask you to hold the line, which means 'wait for the person to answer'. If the extension is free, you can speak to the person. If it is engaged, you can hang up or hold until it is free.
Sami:	The honeymoon is in Florida … for two weeks.		
Gary:	That's great. Congratulations, and good luck in your new life!		
Sami:	Thanks very much. Would you like to come to the marriage?		
Gary:	You mean the wedding.		
Sami:	Do I?	Presenter:	**Lesson 2:** Speaking
Gary:	Yes. Wedding is the ceremony. It's the time when you get married. Marriage is the idea – two people together for the rest of their life.		**B 1 Listen to a call. What's the problem?**
		Abdulla:	Hello?
		Chris:	Good morning. Is that Mohammed?
Sami:	I see. So, would you like to come to the … wedding?	Abdulla:	No, it isn't.
Gary:	I'd love to. When is it?	Chris:	Is Mohammed there?
Sami:	It's on Saturday the sixth at 5.00, but the party starts at 6.00.	Abdulla:	Sorry. I think you've got the wrong number. This is a private house.
Gary:	It's called a reception.	Chris:	Oh. Is that 506-784?
Sami:	Re-cep-tion. Like in a hotel?	Abdulla:	No, sorry.
Gary:	Yes, it's the same word, but it's got two meanings. It also means a party after a wedding.	Chris:	Oh, I'm sorry.
		Abdulla:	It's OK. Bye.
Sami:	Oh. OK. So the … reception starts at 6.00.	Chris:	Goodbye.
Gary:	Where is it?	Presenter:	**B 4 Listen again and check your ideas.**
Sami:	At the Intercontinental Hotel.		[REPEAT OF LESSON 2 EXERCISE B1]
Gary:	Do I need an invitation?	Presenter:	**C 2 Listen and check your ideas.**
Sami:	No, no. Just come along at six.	Abdulla:	Hello?
Gary:	Six on the sixth. Thank you. Thank you very much. I'm really looking forward to it.	Gerald:	Good morning. Is that 506-748?
		Abdulla:	That's right.
Presenter:	**D 2 Listen again and check.**	Gerald:	Is that Abdulla?
	[REPEAT OF LESSON 2 EXERCISE B]	Abdulla:	Yes, speaking.
Presenter:	**Lesson 4:** Applying new skills	Gerald:	Oh, hi, Abdulla. This is Gerald, Khalid's friend.
	B 1 Listen and complete the text with a word or phrase in each space.	Abdulla:	Hi, Gerald.
		Gerald:	I have a message for you from Khalid.
Sami:	I was talking to Gary the other day about weddings in Britain. Apparently, the man is called the groom and the woman is the bride.	Abdulla:	Oh, right.
		Gerald:	He says he can't come to the lecture this morning but he'll see you tomorrow.
Ari:	Really? Do they have a party after the wedding, like we do?	Abdulla:	OK. Thanks for the message.
		Gerald:	Don't mention it. Oh, could you ring Gary and tell him? I don't have his telephone number.
Sami:	Yes, they use the word *reception* for the party.	Abdulla:	Of course.
Ari:	Like the first office in a college?	Gerald:	Thanks. Bye.
Sami:	Yes, I understand that they use the same word for a wedding party.	Presenter:	**E Listen to Abdulla's call. What happens? Why?**
Ari:	And do they go on holiday afterwards?	Mother:	506-930.
Sami:	Yes. They call it a honeymoon. At one time a lot of couples ran away for a month – *moon* means *month* – until the bride's father was sweet again. Nowadays, honeymoons are usually much shorter.	Abdulla:	Hi, this is Abdulla. Is Gary there?
		Mother:	No, I'm sorry. I'm afraid he's out. This is his mother.
		Abdulla:	Oh. Hi.
		Mother:	Can I take a message?
Presenter:	**Theme 7: They Made Our World, Can You Speak Telephone?**	Abdulla:	Yes, please. Could you tell him that Khalid can't come to the lecture this afternoon?
	Lesson 1: Vocabulary	Mother:	Sorry. Could you repeat that?
	B Read and listen to Text 1. It contains some of the green words. Complete Figure 1 with a green word or words in each space.	Abdulla:	Yes, of course. Tell him Khalid can't come to the lecture.
		Mother:	Hamed is coming to the doctor?
Voice:	The telephone is a wonderful invention. It is easy to make a telephone call, but do you know how to talk about it in English?	Abdulla:	No. Khalid can't come to the lecture.
		Mother:	I'm sorry. I can't hear you very well. Could you speak up?
	First you pick up the receiver. You hear the dial tone. You dial the number. If the line is free, you hear the ringing tone until someone answers. If the line is engaged, you hear the engaged tone. You have to hang up and call again later.	Abdulla:	Khalid can't come … Look, never mind. Just ask Gary to call me.
		Mother:	Sorry. What did you say?
		Abdulla:	Ask him … Forget it. I'll call back.
		Mother:	Tell him to call Jack?
Presenter:	**C Read and listen to Text 2. It contains some more green words. Draw a figure to show the information in this text.**	Abdulla:	No … look … Goodbye.
		Presenter:	**Lesson 4:** Applying new skills

B 1 Listen once straight through. Who does Gurkan talk to? Make a list.
Conversation 1

Telephonist: Good morning. Golden Trading Company.
Gurkan: Good morning. I'd like to speak to the General Manager, please.
Telephonist: I'm sorry. I'm afraid he's out. Can anyone else help?
Gurkan: Yes, OK. Could you put me through to Gary Bridges?
Telephonist: Gary Bridges. Do you know his extension number by any chance?
Gurkan: No, I'm afraid I don't.
Telephonist: Please hold the line.
Gurkan: Thank you.
Telephonist: I'm putting you through.
Gurkan: Thanks.

Presenter: **Conversation 2**
Gary: Hello. Gary Bridges speaking.
Gurkan: Hi. Gary. It's Gurkan.
Gary: Hello, Gurkan. How are you?
Gurkan: I'm fine. I'm trying to get hold of the General Manager.
Gary: Oh. He's out at the moment.
Gurkan: Oh, dear. It's quite urgent.
Gary: Well, if you leave a message with his secretary, he will get it as soon as he gets back.
Gurkan: OK. Do you know her extension number?
Gary: No, it's OK. I can put you through from here.
Gurkan: Thanks.
Gary: OK. See you soon, Gurkan. Hold the line.
Gurkan: Thanks.

Presenter: **Conversation 3**
Secretary: Good morning. The General Manager's secretary.
Gurkan: Good morning. I'd like to leave a message for the General Manager.
Secretary: Certainly, sir. Could you give me your name?
Gurkan: Gurkan Uzan.
Secretary: Could you spell that, please?
Gurkan: G-U-R-K-A-N U-Z-A-N.
Secretary: Which company are you from, Mr. Uzan?
Gurkan: General Goods Company.
Secretary: Thank you. And the message?
Gurkan: Could you tell him the meeting at Tiger Engineering tomorrow morning is cancelled?
Secretary: Sorry. Where did you say?
Gurkan: Tiger Engineering.
Secretary: OK. The meeting is cancelled.
Gurkan: Yes. Please can he call me to arrange another time?
Secretary: Please call. OK.
Gurkan: Can you mark the message urgent?
Secretary: Yes, of course. Could you give me your telephone number?
Gurkan: Of course. I'll give you two numbers. My office phone is 506-832.
Secretary: 506-832.
Gurkan: And my mobile is 077-99-403-781.
Secretary: Sorry. Could you repeat that?
Gurkan: 077-99-403-781.
Secretary: OK. Can I read back the message? The meeting at Tiger Engineering tomorrow morning is cancelled. Please call you to arrange another meeting. This is urgent.
Gurkan: That's right. Thank you.
Secretary: Thank you for calling.

Presenter: **B 2 Listen to Conversation 1 again. Say the next word in each pause.**
Conversation 1

Telephonist: Good morning. Golden Trading Company.
Gurkan: Good morning. I'd like to speak to the General [PAUSE] Manager, please.
Telephonist: I'm sorry. I'm afraid he's out. Can anyone else help?
Gurkan: Yes, OK. Could you put me [PAUSE] through to Gary Bridges?
Telephonist: Gary Bridges. Do you know his extension number by any chance?
Gurkan: No, I'm afraid I [PAUSE] don't.
Telephonist: Please hold the line.
Gurkan: Thank [PAUSE] you.
Telephonist: I'm putting you through.
Gurkan: Thanks.

Presenter: **B 3 Listen to Conversation 2 again. Complete Gurkan's sentences in each pause.**
Conversation 2

Gary: Hello. Gary Bridges speaking.
Gurkan: Hi. Gary. It's [PAUSE] Gurkan.
Gary: Hello, Gurkan. How are you?
Gurkan: I'm fine. I'm trying to [PAUSE] get hold of the General Manager.
Gary: Oh. He's out at the moment.
Gurkan: Oh, dear. It's [PAUSE] quite urgent.
Gary: Well, if you leave a message with his secretary, he will get it as soon as he gets back.
Gurkan: OK. Do you know [PAUSE] her extension number?
Gary: No, it's OK. I can put you through from here.
Gurkan: Thanks.
Gary: OK. See you soon, Gurkan. Hold the line.
Gurkan: Thanks.

Presenter: **B 4 Listen to Conversation 3 again. Take Gurkan's message on the first form.**
[REPEAT OF LESSON 4 EXERCISE B1 CONVERSATION 3]

Presenter: **Theme 8: Art and Literature, Joha and His Neighbour**
Lesson 2: Speaking
C 3 Listen and check your ideas.

Narrator: Joha borrowed a small pot from his neighbour. He didn't return the pot the next day, so his neighbour went round.
"Please may I have my small pot back?" he said.
"Of course," said Joha. "Here you are." Joha gave the man his small pot and another tiny one.
"What's this?" said the other man.
"Your small pot had a baby while it was in my house," said Joha.
The neighbour was surprised, but he didn't say anything. He just took the small pot and the tiny pot and went home.
A few days later, Joha borrowed a big pot from his neighbour. He didn't take it back the following afternoon, so the man went to see him.
"Could you give me my big pot back?" he said.
"Certainly," said Joha. "Here you are." Joha handed the man his big pot and another small pot.
"What's this?" said the neighbour.
"Your big pot had a baby while it was with me," said Joha.
The neighbour was delighted and took his big pot and the small pot and went back to his house.
A few days later, Joha borrowed a huge pot from his neighbour. He didn't bring it back the following day, so his neighbour visited him.

"I'd like my huge pot back, please," he said.
"I'm sorry," said Joha. "Your pot died while I was using it."

Presenter: **Theme 9: Sports and Leisure, How Do You Play Surakarta?**
Lesson 1: Vocabulary
B Read and listen to the text.

Voice: F1 Racing
The game
F1 Racing is a game for two, three or four players, with all the fun of real car racing!
Contents
1 playing board, 4 playing pieces (1 red car, 1 blue car, 1 green car, 1 yellow car), 1 spinner
Object
You must get round the track faster than your opponents. Each race is ten times round the track.
How to play
1 Each player must put his or her playing piece on the starting grid.
2 Each player in turn has a go. The player spins the spinner and moves the number of squares.
3 If a playing piece lands on the same square as an opponent's piece, that player must miss the next turn.
4 If a player gets a six, he or she can spin again.

Presenter: **Lesson 2:** Speaking
C Mino is talking to her friend Munira. Listen to the first part of their conversation. Answer the questions.

Mino: Hi, Munira. Happy birthday!
Munira: Thanks very much.
Mino: Here's your present.
Munira: Oh, you shouldn't have.
Mino: Don't be silly. Are you doing anything special?
Munira: Yes. I'm going out for a meal with my family this evening.
Mino: That's great. Where are you going?
Munira: The new Lebanese restaurant in the Garden Mall …

Presenter: D Munira is opening her present from Mino. Listen to the second part of the conversation and complete the first section of the information leaflet – *The game*.

Munira: This looks interesting. What is it?
Mino: It's a board game.
Munira: What do you mean, a board game? Do you play it when you are bored?
Mino: No. Board is spelt B-O-A-R-D, not B-O-R-E-D. You play it on a playing board. It's called *Surakarta*.
Munira: It's called what?
Mino: *Surakarta*. Look. It's on the playing board. Apparently it's from Indonesia, from the island of Java.
Munira: So how do you play it?
Mino: I don't know. Let's read the rules now.
Munira: OK.

Presenter: E Listen to the third part.
Mino: Right. You read out the rules and I'll move the pieces.
Munira: OK. First, let's check the contents. You should have a playing board and 24 counters – 12 red and 12 blue.
Mino: Two four six eight … yes, 12 red and 12 blue. So how do I win the game?
Munira: You must take all my pieces.
Mino: I see. How do we start?
Munira: Right. First rule. Each player must place his or her counters on the first two rows of his or her side of the board.
Mino: The first two rows. I don't understand. There are only 10 squares on the first two rows, but each player has 12 counters.
Munira: Hang on. There's a bit more. Each counter must be on a corner or cross-point.
Mino: Oh, I see. There are six points on each row. OK. I understand now.
Munira: Second rule. Players take turns to move one of their counters.
Mino: What does it mean – take turns?
Munira: It means you have a go and then I have a go.
Mino: Right. How many spaces can I move?
Munira: One space.
Mino: Can I move backwards?
Munira: Yes, you can. Forwards, backwards or diagonally.
Mino: What happens if there is another counter on that space? Can I jump over a counter or take it?
Munira: No, you can't jump over it and you can't land on an occupied space.
Mino: So how can I take your pieces?
Munira: You can move along a line of unoccupied spaces, but you must go round at least one loop.
Mino: What's a loop?
Munira: One of these things here at the corners.
Mino: This looks like fun. Let's play a game.
Munira: OK. You go first …

Presenter: F 2 Listen again and check your ideas.
[REPEAT OF LESSON 2 EXERCISE E]

Presenter: **Theme 10: Nutrition and Health, Truths and Myths**
Lesson 2: Speaking review (1)
B 2 Listen to the first part of the conversation and check your ideas.

Vera: Hi, Fatima. How are you?
Fatima: I'm OK.
Vera: What's the matter?
Fatima: Nothing, really.
Vera: Come on. Tell me what's wrong.

Presenter: C In this course you have learnt to talk about arrangements. Listen to the second part of the conversation. What arrangements does Fatima talk about?

Fatima: Really, it's nothing. I'm just bored. I arranged to meet Munira this evening, but she phoned and left me a message while I was out. It seems that she can't come now.
Vera: Oh, dear. Why not?
Fatima: Her parents are having a party and they want her to be there. Apparently, all her relatives are coming. I understand that her brother is flying in from Qatar.
Vera: I see.

Presenter: D 2 Listen to the second part of the conversation again and check.
[REPEAT OF LESSON 2 EXERCISE C]

Presenter: E 1 Listen to the third part of the conversation. What new phrase does Fatima learn?

Vera: Well, I've got just the thing to cheer you up.
Fatima: To what?
Vera: To cheer you up.
Fatima: What does it mean?

Vera:	It means 'to make you happy'.
Fatima:	Chair you up?
Vera:	No, cheer. Cheer you up.
Fatima:	OK. So, what have you got to cheer me up?
Presenter:	**F 1 Listen to the fourth part of the conversation. What does Vera think about the first three statements in the quiz? What about Fatima?**
Fatima:	I don't like playing board games.
Vera:	No, it's not a board game. It's a quiz. In this magazine.
Fatima:	What's it about?
Vera:	It's about your hair, your eyes, your skin and your teeth.
Fatima:	What about them?
Vera:	There are lots of statements. We must decide if each one is true or false.
Fatima:	Go on then. Read one out.
Vera:	OK. Your hair. Do you think washing damages your hair?
Fatima:	Yes, I think it does.
Vera:	Yes, so do I. So I'll put a tick under Me and another one under You.
Fatima:	What's the next one?
Vera:	If you cut your hair, it will grow faster. Do you think that's true?
Fatima:	No, I don't. I think that's nonsense.
Vera:	I don't know. It might be true. So I'll put a question mark for me and a cross for you. Number 3: You can repair split ends with the right shampoo.
Fatima:	What are split ends?
Vera:	You know, when your hair divides into two at the end.
Fatima:	Oh yes. What's the statement again?
Vera:	You can repair split ends with the right shampoo.
Fatima:	No, I don't think that's true.
Vera:	Don't you? I do. The adverts always say: 'This shampoo repairs split ends.'
Fatima:	Of course they do. They want you to buy the shampoo, don't they? But I don't think you can repair … what are they called again?
Vera:	Split ends.
Fatima:	Right. I don't think you can repair split ends.
Vera:	OK. Well I disagree with you. I think you can. So I'll put a tick for me and a cross for you. Right. Number 4.